teacher's friend publications

July & Aug.

a creative idea book
for the
elementary teacher

written and illustrated
by
Karen Sevaly

Reproduction of these materials for commercial resale or distribution to an entire school or school district is strictly prohibited. Pages may be duplicated for one individual classroom set only. Material may not be reproduced for other purposes without the prior written permission of the publisher.

Copyright © 1989
Teacher's Friend Publications, Inc.
All rights reserved
Printed in the United States of America
Published by Teacher's Friend Publications, Inc.
7407 Orangewood Drive, Riverside, CA 92504

ISBN 0-943263-10-7

 TO TEACHERS AND CHILDREN EVERYWHERE.

A Special Index to All Teacher's Friend Idea Books included in this Edition!

Table of Contents

MAKING THE MOST OF IT! 7

    What is in this book 8
    How to use this book 8
    Adding the color 9
    Laminators 9
    Ditto masters 10
    Bulletin boards 11
    On-going bulletin boards 11
    Lettering and headings 12

CALENDARS - JULY & AUGUST 15

    July calendar and activities 16
    July calendar topper 19
    July blank calendar 20
    August calendar and activities 21
    August calendar topper 24
    August blank calendar 25
    Mini calendar symbols 26

SUMMER ACTIVITIES AND GETTING READY 27

    Summer awards 28
    Bookmarks 29
    Pencil toppers 30
    My summer book 31
    Summer writing 32
    Ice cream cones 33
    Keys to success 34
    Shoe pattern 35
    School bus gameboard 36
    Good conduct contract 38
    Welcome back letter 39
    Name mobiles 40
    Super student award 41
    International children - U.S.A. 42
    Pencil writing 44

4th OF JULY 45

    Independence Day 46
    My liberty book 47
    Patriotic fun 48
    Eagle puppet 49
    We the people 50
    4th of July - visor 51
    Uncle Sam 52
    The Great Seal of the U.S.A. 53
    Creative writing 54

OUR SOLAR SYSTEM ... 55

- Space fun ... 57
- Martian mania ... 58
- Solar system bingo ... 58
- Astronaut wheel ... 60
- My space book ... 62
- Mr. Sun puppet ... 63
- Solar system mobile ... 64
- Star puzzle ... 67
- My space shuttle book ... 68
- Space award ... 69
- Space writing ... 70

NUTRITION ... 71

- Summer recipes ... 72
- Four basic food groups ... 73
- Food group card game ... 74
- Important nutrients ... 76
- Recipe cards ... 77
- Nutritious candy bar ... 78
- Hamburger mobile ... 79
- Bunch of grapes puppet ... 80
- Pizza award ... 81
- Food group characters ... 82
- My weekly diet ... 84

TRAVEL AND TRANSPORTATION ... 85

- Travel activities ... 86
- Travel bingo ... 86
- Transportation fun ... 88
- My trip record ... 89
- Traveling story starters ... 90
- Safety first ... 92
- School bus book ... 93
- School bus rules ... 94
- Spiral helicopter ... 95
- Creative writing ... 96

BULLETIN BOARDS AND MORE! ... 97

- July & August bulletin boards ... 98
- Liberty bell pattern ... 101
- Wishful thinking ... 102
- Classroom signs ... 103

ANSWER KEY ... 109

SPECIAL INDEX FOR ALL MONTHLY CREATIVE IDEA BOOKS ... 111

Making the Most of It!

WHAT IS IN
THIS BOOK:

You will find the following in each monthly idea book from Teacher's Friend Publications:

1. A calendar listing every day of the month with a classroom idea.

2. At least four new student awards to be sent home to parents.

3. Three new bookmarks that can be used in your school library or given to students by you as "Super Student Awards."

4. Numerous bulletin board ideas and patterns pertaining to the particular month.

5. Easy to make craft ideas related to the monthly holidays.

6. Dozens of activities emphasizing not only the obvious holidays but also chapters related to such subjects as; Our Solar System and Nutrition.

7. Crossword puzzles, word finds, creative writing pages, booklet covers, games and much more.

8. Scores of classroom management techniques, the newest and the best.

HOW TO USE
THIS BOOK:

Every page of this book may be duplicated for individual classroom use.

Some pages are meant to be used as duplicating masters and used as student work sheets. Other pages may be copied onto construction paper or used as they are.

If you have access to a print shop, you will find that many pages work well when printed on index paper. This type of paper takes crayons and felt markers well and is sturdy enough to last and last. (The bookmarks work particularly well on index paper.)

Lastly, some pages are meant to be enlarged with an overhead or opaque projector. When we say enlarge, we mean it! Think BIG! Three, four or even five feet is great! Try using colored butcher paper or poster board so you don't spend all your time coloring.

Making the Most of It!

ADDING THE COLOR:

Putting the color to finished items can be a real bother to teachers in a rush. Try these ideas:

1. On small areas, water color markers work great. If your area is rather large switch to crayons or even colored chalk or pastels.

   (Don't worry, lamination or a spray fixative will keep the color on the work and off of you. No laminator or fixative? That's okay, a little hair spray will do the trick.)

2. The quickest method of coloring large items is to simply start with colored paper. (Poster board, butcher paper and large construction paper work well.) Add a few dashes of a contrasting colored marker or crayon and you will have it made.

3. Try cutting character eyes, teeth, etc. from white typing paper and gluing them in place. These features will really stand out and make your bulletin boards come alive.

   For special effects add real buttons or lace. Metallic paper looks great on stars and belt buckles, too.

LAMINATORS:

If you have access to a roll laminator you already know how fortunate you are. They are priceless when it comes to saving time and money. Try these ideas:

1. You can laminate more than just classroom posters and construction paper. Try various kinds of fabric, wall paper and gift wrapping. You'll be surprised at the great combinations you come up with.

   Laminated classified ads can be used to cut headings for current event bulletin boards. Colorful gingham fabric makes terrific cut letters or scalloped edging. You might even try burlap! It looks terrific on a fall bulletin board.

   (You can even make professional looking bookmarks with laminated fabric or burlap. They are great gift ideas.)

2. Felt markers and laminated paper or fabric can work as a team. Just make sure the markers you use are permanent and not water based. Oops, make a mistake! That's okay. Put a little ditto fluid on a tissue, rub across the mark and presto, it's gone! (Dry transfer markers work great on lamination, too.)

"TEACHER'S FRIEND" ©   JULY & AUGUST

Making the Most of It!

LAMINATORS: (continued)

3. Laminating cut-out characters can be tricky. If you have enlarged an illustration onto poster board, simply laminate first and then cut it out with an art knife. (Just make sure the laminator is plenty hot.)

   One problem may arise when you paste an illustration onto poster board and laminate the finished product. If your paste-up does not cover 100% of the illustration, the poster board may separate from it after laminating. To avoid this problem, paste your illustration onto poster board that measures slightly larger. This way, the lamination will help hold down your illustration.

4. Have you ever laminated student made place mats, crayon shavings, tissue paper collages, or dried flowers? You'll be amazed at the variety of creative things that can be laminated and used in the classroom, or as take-home gifts.

DITTO MASTERS:

Many of the pages in this book can be made into masters for duplicating. Try some of these ideas for best results:

1. When using new masters, turn down the pressure on the duplicating machine. As the copies become light, increase the pressure. This will get longer wear out of both the master and the machine.

2. If the print from the back side of your original comes through the front when making a master or photocopy, slip a sheet of black construction paper behind the sheet. This will mask the unwanted black lines and create a much better copy.

3. Trying to squeeze one more run out of that worn master can be frustrating. Try lightly spraying the inked side of the master with hair spray. For some reason, this helps the master put out those few extra copies.

4. Several potential masters in this book contain instructions for the teacher. Simply cover the type with correction fluid or a small slip of paper before duplicating.

"TEACHER'S FRIEND" ©   JULY & AUGUST

Making the Most of It!

BULLETIN BOARDS:

Creating clever bulletin boards for your classroom need not take fantastic amounts of time and money. With a little preparation and know-how you can have different boards each month with very little effort. Try some of these ideas:

1. Background paper should be put up only once a year. Choose colors that can go with many themes and holidays. A black butcher paper background will look terrific with springtime butterflies or a spooky Halloween display.

2. Butcher paper is not the only thing that can be used to cover the back of your board. You might like to try the classified ad section of the local newspaper for a current events board. Or how about colored burlap? Just fold it up at the end of the year to reuse again.

3. Wallpaper is another great background cover. Discontinued rolls can be purchased for next to nothing at discount hardware stores. Most can be wiped clean and will not fade like construction paper. (Do not glue wallpaper directly to the board, just staple or pin in place.)

ON-GOING BULLETIN BOARDS:

Creating the on-going bulletin board can be easy. Give one of these ideas a try.

1. Choose one board to be a calendar display. Students can change this monthly. They can do the switching of dates, month titles and holiday symbols. Start the year with a great calendar board and with a few minor changes each month it will add a sparkle to the classroom.

2. A classroom tree bulletin board is another one that requires very little attention after September. Cut a large bare tree from brown butcher paper and display it in the center of the board. (Wood-grained adhesive paper makes a great tree, also.) Children can add fall leaves, flowers, apples, Christmas ornaments, birds, valentines, etc., to change the appearance each month.

"TEACHER'S FRIEND" ©   JULY & AUGUST

Making the Most of It!

ON-GOING BULLETIN BOARDS: (continued)

3. Birthday bulletin boards, classroom helpers, school announcement displays and reading group charts can all be created once before school starts and changed monthly with very little effort. With all these on-going ideas, you'll discover that all that bulletin board space seems smaller than you thought.

LETTERING AND HEADINGS:

Not every school has a letter machine that produces perfect 2" or 4" letters from construction paper. (There is such a thing, you know.) The rest of us will just have to use the old stencil and scissor method. But wait, there is an easier way!

1. Don't cut individual letters. They are difficult to pin up straight, anyway. Instead, hand print bulletin board titles and headings onto strips of colored paper. When it is time for the board to come down, simply roll it up to use again next year.

   Use your imagination. Try cloud shapes and cartoon bubbles. They will all look great.

2. Hand lettering is not that difficult, even if your printing is not up to penmanship standards. Print block letters with a felt marker. Draw big dots at the ends of each letter. This will hide any mistakes and add a charming touch to the overall effect.

"TEACHER'S FRIEND" ©   JULY & AUGUST

Making the Most of It!

LETTERING AND
HEADINGS:
(continued)

If you are still afraid about free handing it, try this nifty idea: Cut a strip of poster board about 28" X 6". Down the center of the strip cut a window with an art knife measuring 20" X 2". There you have it, a perfect stencil for any lettering job. All you do is write your letters with a felt marker within the window slot. Don't worry about uniformity, just fill up the entire window heighth with your letters. Move your poster board strip along as you go. The letters will always remain straight and even because the poster board window is straight.

3. If you must cut individual letters, use this idea:

Cut numerous sheets of construction paper into 4½" X 6" squares. (Laminate first if you can.) Cut letters as shown in the illustration. No need to measure, irregular letters will look creative not messy.

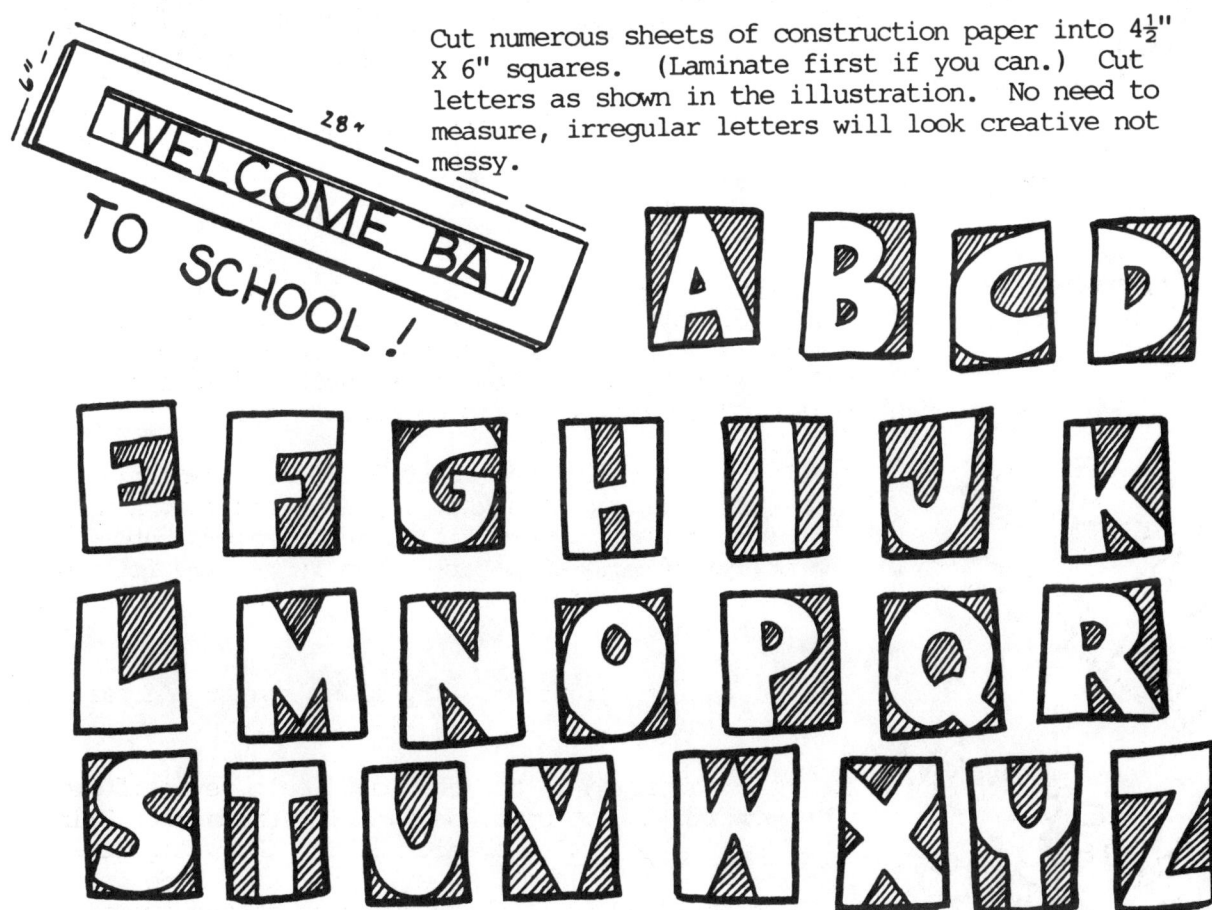

"TEACHER'S FRIEND" ©   JULY & AUGUST

Notes

- JULY CALENDAR
- AUGUST CALENDAR
- CALENDAR TOPPERS
- BLANK CALENDARS
- MINI CALENDAR SYMBOLS

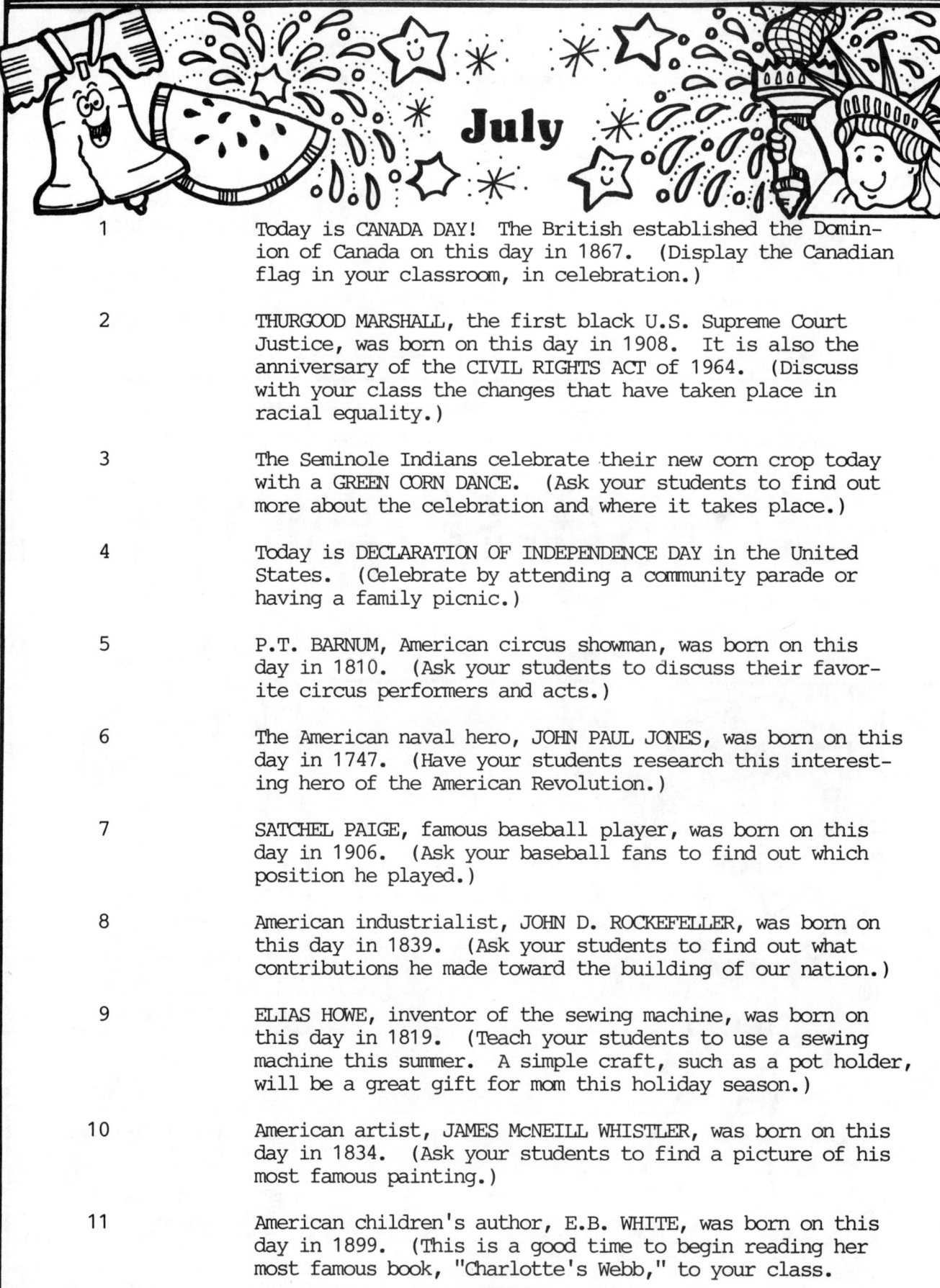

July

1 — Today is CANADA DAY! The British established the Dominion of Canada on this day in 1867. (Display the Canadian flag in your classroom, in celebration.)

2 — THURGOOD MARSHALL, the first black U.S. Supreme Court Justice, was born on this day in 1908. It is also the anniversary of the CIVIL RIGHTS ACT of 1964. (Discuss with your class the changes that have taken place in racial equality.)

3 — The Seminole Indians celebrate their new corn crop today with a GREEN CORN DANCE. (Ask your students to find out more about the celebration and where it takes place.)

4 — Today is DECLARATION OF INDEPENDENCE DAY in the United States. (Celebrate by attending a community parade or having a family picnic.)

5 — P.T. BARNUM, American circus showman, was born on this day in 1810. (Ask your students to discuss their favorite circus performers and acts.)

6 — The American naval hero, JOHN PAUL JONES, was born on this day in 1747. (Have your students research this interesting hero of the American Revolution.)

7 — SATCHEL PAIGE, famous baseball player, was born on this day in 1906. (Ask your baseball fans to find out which position he played.)

8 — American industrialist, JOHN D. ROCKEFELLER, was born on this day in 1839. (Ask your students to find out what contributions he made toward the building of our nation.)

9 — ELIAS HOWE, inventor of the sewing machine, was born on this day in 1819. (Teach your students to use a sewing machine this summer. A simple craft, such as a pot holder, will be a great gift for mom this holiday season.)

10 — American artist, JAMES McNEILL WHISTLER, was born on this day in 1834. (Ask your students to find a picture of his most famous painting.)

11 — American children's author, E.B. WHITE, was born on this day in 1899. (This is a good time to begin reading her most famous book, "Charlotte's Webb," to your class.

July

12 — GEORGE EASTMAN, inventor of the camera and founder of the Eastman Kodak Company, was born on this day in 1854. (Ask your students to each bring in a photo of themselves to display on a class bulletin board.)

13 — The first trans-Atlantic telephone conversation via TELSTAR was completed on this day in 1962. (Students might be interested in knowing how satellite communications work in both television and telephone.)

14 — Today is BASTILLE DAY! A celebration honoring the victory of the people during the French Revolution in 1789. (Ask students to find the city of Paris on the class map.)

15 — REMBRANDT VAN RIJN, famous old master Dutch artist, was born on this day in 1606. (Bring some of Rembrandt's beautiful paintings (prints) into your classroom.)

16 — APOLLO !! is launched in 1969, carrying astronauts Collins, Armstrong and Aldrin. (Ask your students to locate Cape Canaveral, Florida, on your classroom map.)

17 — APOLLO 18 and the U.S.S.R. craft SOYUZ 19 link up in space in a dramatic gesture of goodwill in 1975. (Ask your students what other ways our two countries could promote peace and goodwill.)

18 — JOHN GLENN JR., American astronaut and politician, was born on this day in 1921. (Ask students to find out the particulars of his historic flight.)

19 — The first WOMEN'S RIGHTS CONVENTION was held on this day in Seneca Falls, New York, in 1848. (Ask students to list some rights that women now have that they did not have then.)

20 — The first LANDING ON THE MOON, by American astronauts Neil Armstrong and Buzz Aldrin, was accomplished on this day in 1969. (Ask your students to find out what Armstrong said when he first stepped foot on the moon's surface.)

21 — The British explorer, MUNGO PARK, began his voyage down the Niger River in Africa, on this day in 1796. (Ask your students to trace his route on the class map.)

22 — EMMA LAZARUS, American poet who wrote the poem engraved on the Statue of Liberty, was born on this day in 1849. (Read her famous poem to your students.)

July

23   The ICE CREAM CONE was introduced at the World's Fair in St. Louis by Italo Marchioni, in 1903. (Treat your students to an ice cream treat on this summer day.)

24   Today is MORMON PIONEER DAY, celebrating the founding of their settlement in Salt Lake City, Utah, in 1847. (Have students locate the Great Salt Lake on the classroom map.)

25   Franklin D. Roosevelt was the first president to visit the islands of HAWAII, in 1934. (Discuss the customs and dress of the people of Hawaii and hold a class luau.)

26   NEW YORK STATE becomes the eleventh state to ratify the constitution and become a state, on this day in 1788. (Ask your students to name the other twelve states that made up the original thirteen.)

27   U.S. figure skater, PEGGY FLEMING, was born on this day in 1948. (Ask your students to find out which year she won her Olympic gold medal.)

28   British children's author, BEATRIX POTTER, was born on this day in 1866. (Read one of her charming stories to your class during quiet time.)

29   CHARLES, PRINCE OF WALES and LADY DIANA SPENCER were married in St. Paul's Cathedral, in London, on this day in 1981. (See if your students know the identities of these two people.)

30   HENRY FORD, American automobile manufacturer, was born on this day in 1863. (Ask your students to design a car that they might like to see developed for the future.)

31   THOMAS EDISON received a U.S. patent on his phonograph, on this day in 1877. (Ask students what they think about the progress in this technology and how it might change in the future.)

July

sun	mon	tue	wed	thu	fri	sat

August

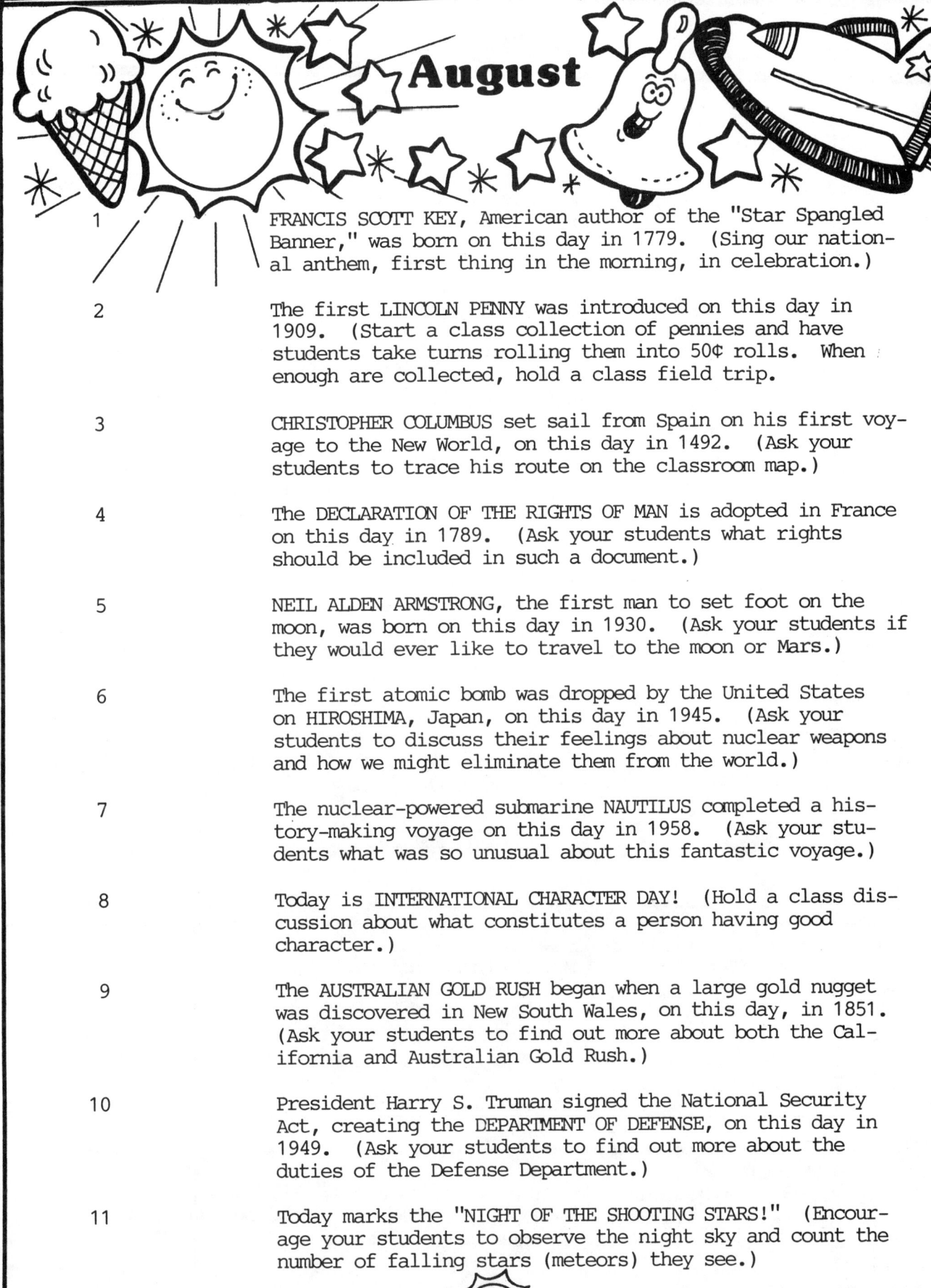

1. FRANCIS SCOTT KEY, American author of the "Star Spangled Banner," was born on this day in 1779. (Sing our national anthem, first thing in the morning, in celebration.)

2. The first LINCOLN PENNY was introduced on this day in 1909. (Start a class collection of pennies and have students take turns rolling them into 50¢ rolls. When enough are collected, hold a class field trip.

3. CHRISTOPHER COLUMBUS set sail from Spain on his first voyage to the New World, on this day in 1492. (Ask your students to trace his route on the classroom map.)

4. The DECLARATION OF THE RIGHTS OF MAN is adopted in France on this day in 1789. (Ask your students what rights should be included in such a document.)

5. NEIL ALDEN ARMSTRONG, the first man to set foot on the moon, was born on this day in 1930. (Ask your students if they would ever like to travel to the moon or Mars.)

6. The first atomic bomb was dropped by the United States on HIROSHIMA, Japan, on this day in 1945. (Ask your students to discuss their feelings about nuclear weapons and how we might eliminate them from the world.)

7. The nuclear-powered submarine NAUTILUS completed a history-making voyage on this day in 1958. (Ask your students what was so unusual about this fantastic voyage.)

8. Today is INTERNATIONAL CHARACTER DAY! (Hold a class discussion about what constitutes a person having good character.)

9. The AUSTRALIAN GOLD RUSH began when a large gold nugget was discovered in New South Wales, on this day, in 1851. (Ask your students to find out more about both the California and Australian Gold Rush.)

10. President Harry S. Truman signed the National Security Act, creating the DEPARTMENT OF DEFENSE, on this day in 1949. (Ask your students to find out more about the duties of the Defense Department.)

11. Today marks the "NIGHT OF THE SHOOTING STARS!" (Encourage your students to observe the night sky and count the number of falling stars (meteors) they see.)

"TEACHER'S FRIEND" ©   JULY & AUGUST

August

12   KATHERINE LEE BATES, author of the poem "America the Beautiful" was born on this day in 1859. (Ask your students to write their own poem about America.)

13   Construction of the BERLIN WALL began on this day in 1961. (Explain to your students how this wall has not only divided the city of Berlin but also many German families.)

14   Today is VICTORY DAY! This day celebrates the ending of World War II with the surrender of the Japanese in 1945. (Ask your students what other days might be considered "Victory Day!")

15   The PANAMA CANAL was opened on this day in 1914. (Locate the canal on the class map and illustrate how it has benefitted world trade and travel.)

16   GAS STREET LIGHTS were introduced for the first time in London on this day in 1807. (Hold a class discussion about what life must have been like in the early 1800's.)

17   The American frontiersman, DAVY CROCKETT, was born on this day in 1786. (Arrange for a showing of Disney's "Davy Crockett" films, in celebration.)

18   VIRGINIA DARE, the first English child born in colonial America, was born on this day in 1587. (Ask your students to find out more about the first group of colonists that came to America.)

19   Today is NATIONAL AVIATION DAY and the birth date of ORVILLE WRIGHT, in 1871. (You might want to invite a pilot to your class to talk about his love of flying.)

20   REINHOLD MESSNER, of Italy, was the first successful solo climber of MT. EVEREST, in 1980. (Ask your students to find out the altitude of the world's highest mountain.)

21   HAWAII becomes the 50th U.S. state on this day in 1959. (Serve your class a treat of fresh pineapple in celebration.)

22   The INTERNATIONAL RED CROSS is established in Geneva, Switzerland, on this day in 1864. (Students might like to contribute, as a class, to this worthwhile organization.

23   American dancer and choreographer, GENE KELLY, was born on this day in 1912. (Encourage your budding dancers to show their talents to the class.)

"TEACHER'S FRIEND" ©   JULY & AUGUST

August

24 — On this day in 79 A.D., MT VESUVIUS erupted in southern Italy. (Older students might like to mark existing volcanos on the classroom map.)

25 — LEONARD BERNSTEIN, American composer and conductor, was born on this day in 1918. (Students might like to listen to his music from "West Side Story" and relate it to teenagers today.)

26 — The 19th AMENDMENT to the U.S. Constitution was ratified on this day in 1920. (Have your students find out what this amendment gave us.)

27 — **Humanitarian**, MOTHER TERESA, was born on this day in 1910. She won a Nobel Peace Prize, in 1979, for her work with the poor in India. (Ask your students to locate India on the classroom map.)

28 — Today marks the anniversary of the MARCH ON WASHINGTON, in 1963. (Find a copy of Martin Luther King's speech "I Have a Dream" and read it to the class.)

29 — American entertainer, MICHAEL JACKSON, was born on this day in 1958. (Your students will love dancing to one of his songs during physical education.)

30 — U.S. Senator, STROM THURMOND, set a filibuster record of speaking for 24 hours, 27 minutes, on this day in 1957. (Ask your students to find out what he talked about.)

31 — The developer of the Montessori method of education, MARIA MONTESSORI, was born on this day in 1870. (Celebrate by simply having a great back to school!)

August

sun	mon	tue	wed	thu	fri	sat

Mini Calendar Symbols

"TEACHER'S FRIEND" ©   26   JULY & AUGUST

Summer Awards

Name _____

WAS A TERRIFIC STUDENT TODAY!

Date _____ Teacher _____

Name _____

WAS A PERFECT STUDENT IN CLASS TODAY!

Date _____ Teacher _____

Name _____

WAS A BIG HELP IN CLASS TODAY!

Date _____
Teacher _____

Date _____

YOU WERE CERTAINLY A JOY IN CLASS TODAY!

Name _____

Teacher _____

"TEACHER'S FRIEND" ©   JULY & AUGUST

Pencil Toppers

Reproduce these "Pencil Toppers" onto construction paper. Color and cut out. Use an art knife to cut through the Xs.

Slide a pencil through both Xs, as shown.

Use as classroom, holiday or birthday treats.

"TEACHER'S FRIEND" ©   JULY & AUGUST

Summer Writing

S
U
M
M
E
R

I love the summer because....

Ice Cream Cones

Make several cones and ice cream patterns from colored construction paper. Place two cone patterns together and staple the sides. Add your own matching problems and have your students match the appropriate ice cream scoop to the correct cone.

Keys to Success

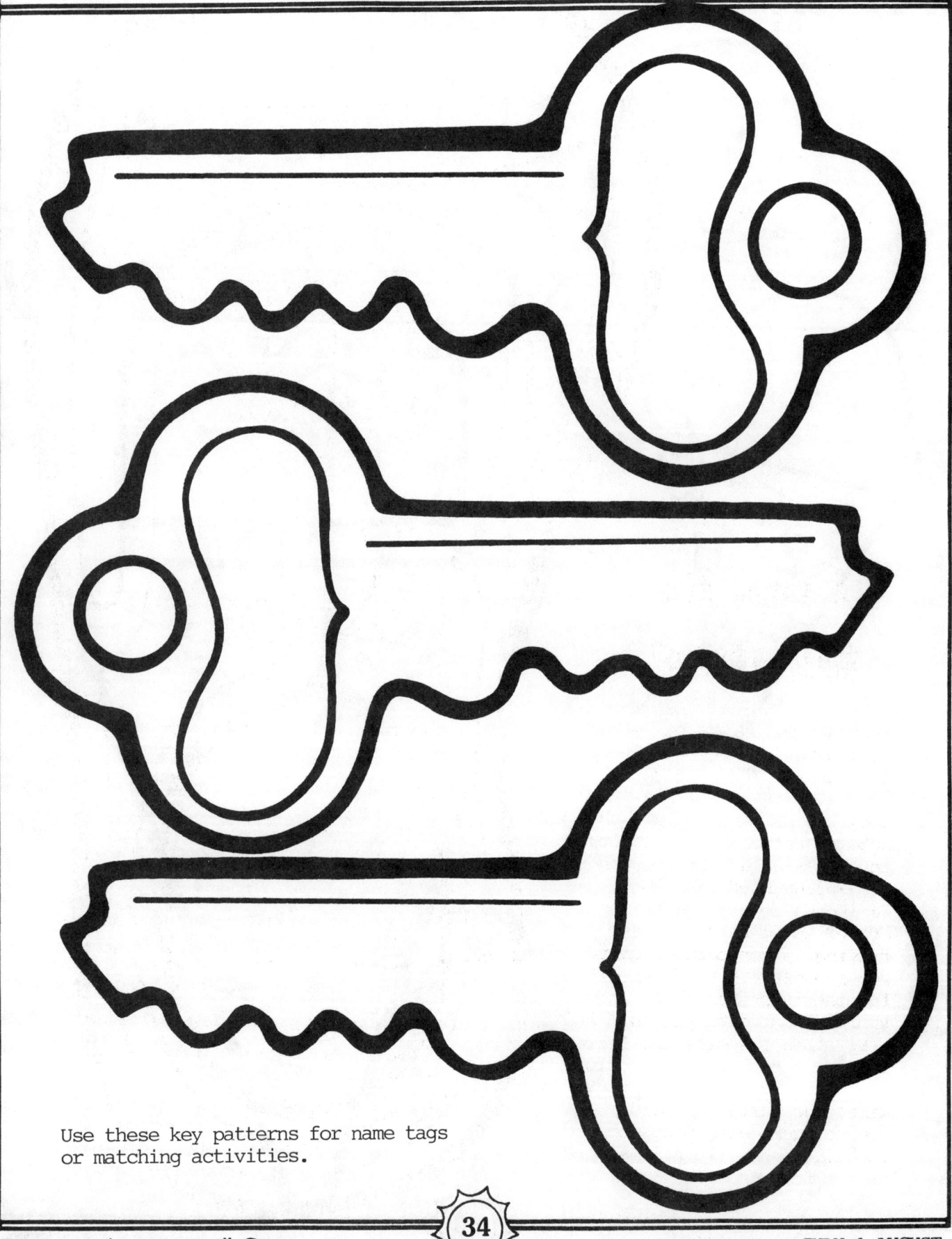

Use these key patterns for name tags or matching activities.

Shoe Pattern

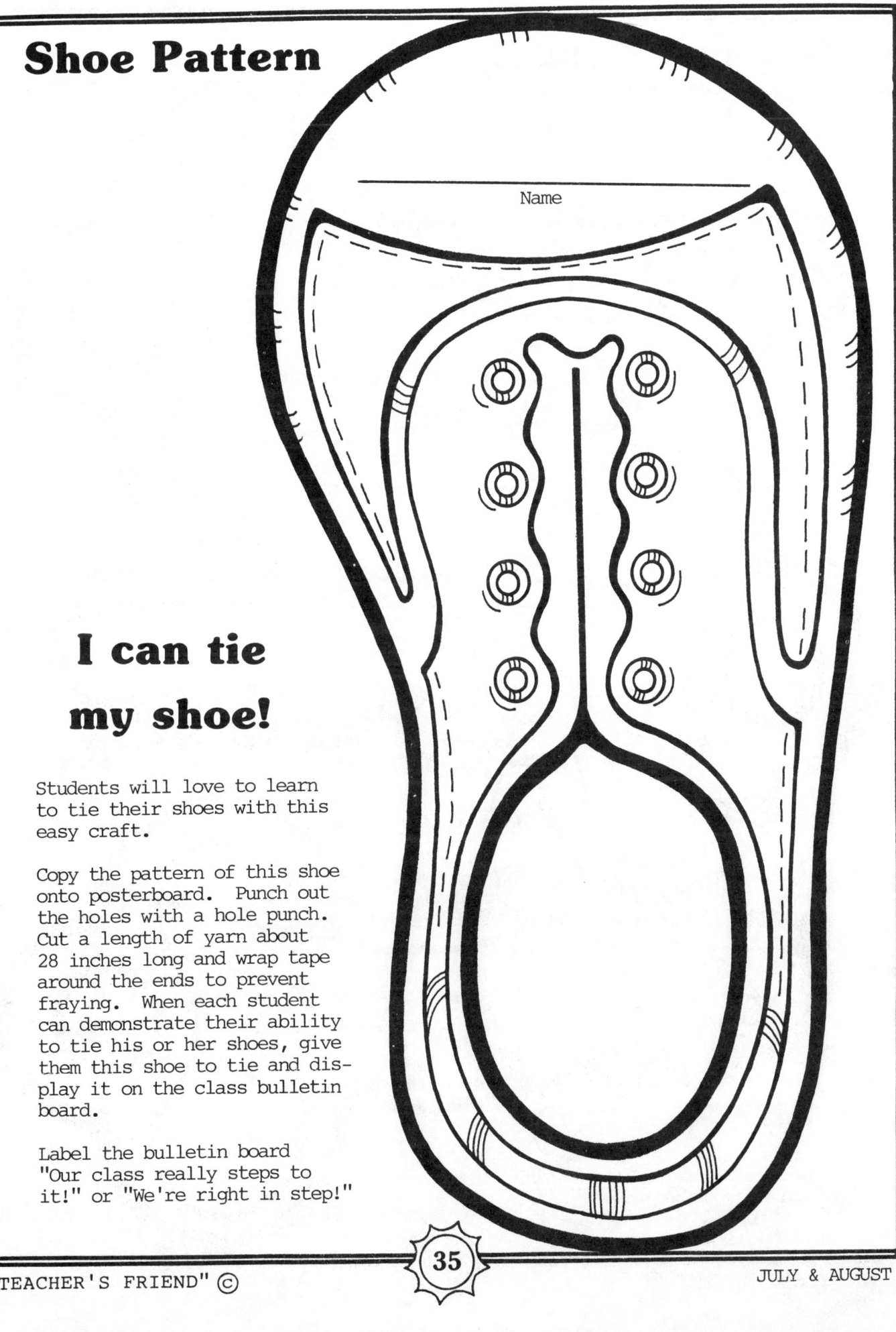

I can tie my shoe!

Students will love to learn to tie their shoes with this easy craft.

Copy the pattern of this shoe onto posterboard. Punch out the holes with a hole punch. Cut a length of yarn about 28 inches long and wrap tape around the ends to prevent fraying. When each student can demonstrate their ability to tie his or her shoes, give them this shoe to tie and display it on the class bulletin board.

Label the bulletin board "Our class really steps to it!" or "We're right in step!"

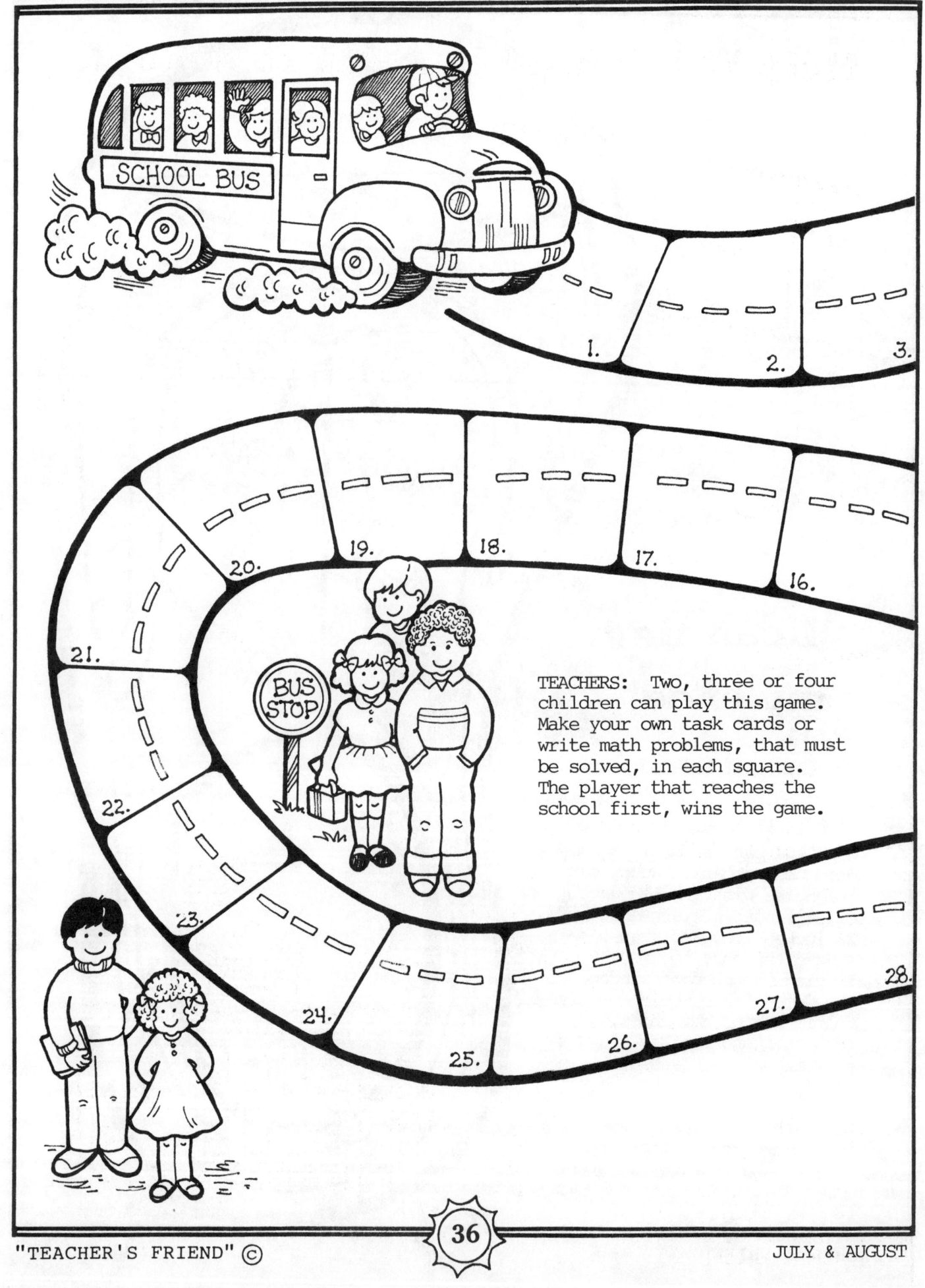

Good Conduct Contract

_____ name

I promise to _____
_____
_____
_____
_____
_____
_____

by this date _____

If I do, I will be rewarded by _____
_____
_____
_____
_____
_____
_____

Student _____

Teacher _____

Parent _____

Welcome Back to School!

_____

Dear _____,

_____
_____
_____
_____
_____
_____
_____
_____
_____
_____
_____
_____
_____
_____
_____

Write a personal letter to each student in class. Tell them about all the great things they can look forward to in the new school year.

Place your school logo over this paragraph.

Sincerely,

_____

"TEACHER'S FRIEND" ©   JULY & AUGUST

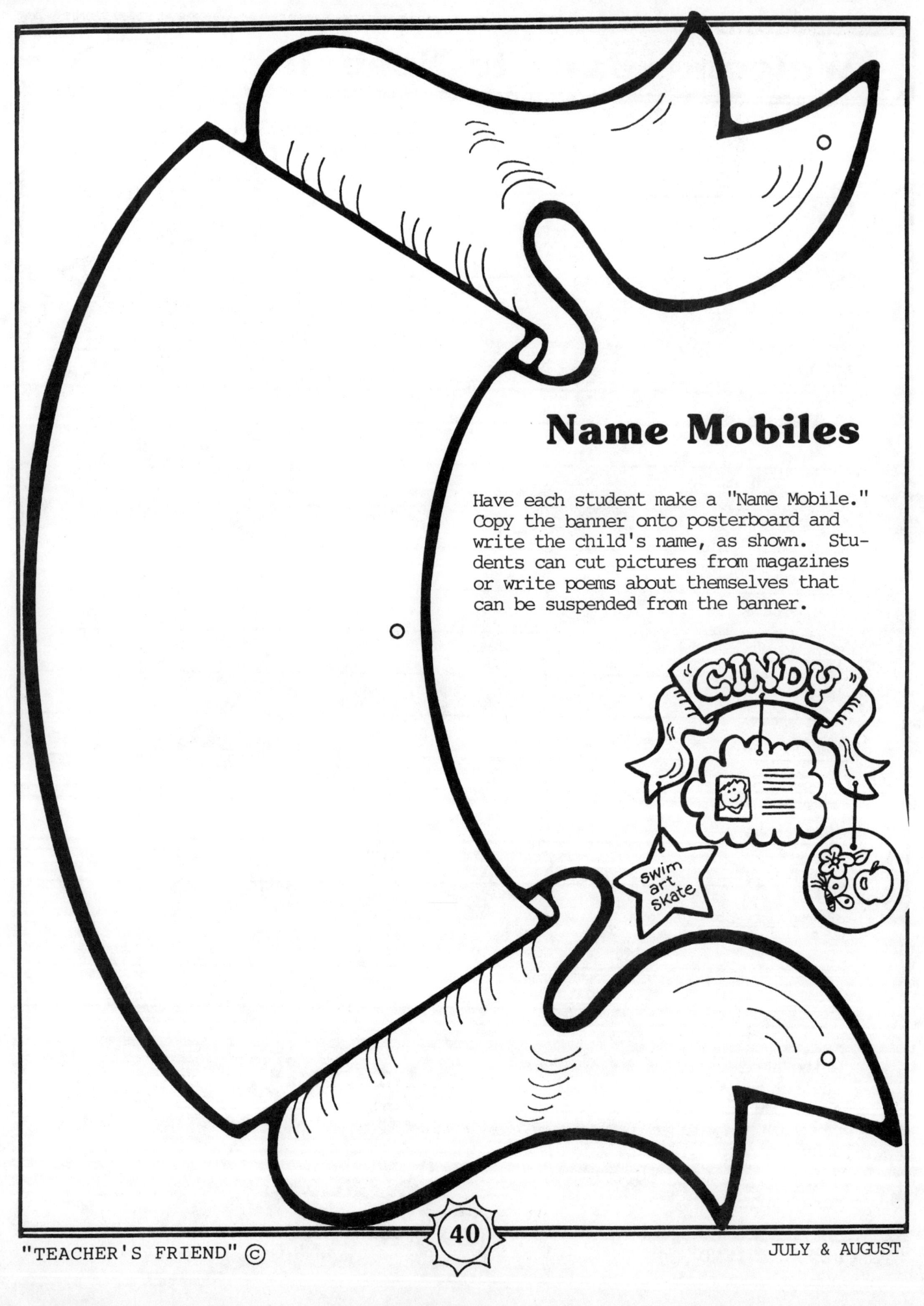

Name Mobiles

Have each student make a "Name Mobile." Copy the banner onto posterboard and write the child's name, as shown. Students can cut pictures from magazines or write poems about themselves that can be suspended from the banner.

International Children

4th of July

- INDEPENDENCE DAY
- MY LIBERTY BOOK
- PATRIOTIC FUN
- EAGLE PUPPET
- "WE THE PEOPLE"
- 4th OF JULY VISOR
- UNCLE SAM
- GREAT SEAL OF THE U.S.

"TEACHER'S FRIEND" ©

JULY & AUGUST

Independence Day

The most important patriotic holiday to all United States citizens is Independence Day, or the Fourth of July. Independence Day celebrates the historical signing of the Declaration Of Independence by the Continental Congress on July 4, 1776. With this act, the thirteen colonies formed a new nation, the United States of America.

Celebrations continued for several days. The people of Philadelphia, Pennsylvania, cheered as the news was spread that the Declaration of Independence had been signed. The Liberty Bell was rung at Independence Hall and a statue of King George III was taken down and destroyed. That night people lit bonfires and danced in the streets in celebration.

Today, the Fourth of July is celebrated with family picnics, parades, fireworks and political speeches. It is a happy, joyous time but also one in which we should all remember the sacrifices our forefathers made in order to give us this great nation.

Declaration of Independence

The Declaration of Independence is a document that declares the rights of a new nation. It explained the feelings of the colonists and listed the wrongs they had suffered under British rule. It also states that the people of the United States will fight their own wars, make their own peace and carry on their own trade. With the signing of this document, the United States became an independent, free nation.

The first person to sign the Declaration was John Hancock, president of the Continental Congress. Thomas Jefferson, with the help of Benjamin Franklin and John Adams, wrote the document. Fifty-six men signed the declaration. In signing, each man pledged to his new country, "our lives, our fortunes, and our sacred honor."

You might like to read a few sentences of the Declaration of Independence to your students.

"We hold these truths to be self-evident, that all men are created equal, that they are endowed by their Creator with certain unalienable Rights, that among these are Life, Liberty and the pursuit of Happiness. That to secure these rights, Governments are instituted among Men, deriving their just powers from the consent of the governed."

Patriotic Fun

FIND THESE PATRIOTIC WORDS:

- INDEPENDENCE
- DECLARATION
- LIBERTY
- JUSTICE
- PATRIOTISM
- STARS
- STRIPES
- UNCLE SAM
- FLAG
- GLORY
- AMERICA
- FREEDOM

```
X C F T R E V F R E E D O M D F T Y U N H
D F L D T Y G H J U S E T E O U L K J H R
F Y A R G T Y J U S T I C E D E W R T Y U
W Q G F G T Y H J U I K L O P H J S R T Y
P A T R I O T I S M S W Q E R T Y T V B N
S D F R T G G D E D S E W D S W T A Y U I
F B V C X L T Y U I L I B E R T Y R E W Q
D C V F G O G T H D E S E S A E T S T U Y
F B V C X R F A M E R I C A D R E T G T U
C V B F G Y D R E F G T H Y U J K R F T R
U N C L E S A M D R F G T Y H J U I D F R
A S D F R E G V B N M J H K I U J P D V B
F G D E C L A R A T I O N D F R T E R G H
D F V G B H N J M K L O I K J M N S F R T
D V B G F B N G G I N D E P E N D E N C E
S C V B H G N M J K L O I K M J N H Y T G
```

ACTIVITY 1

FIND OUT WHO'S HIDING IN THESE NUMBERS!

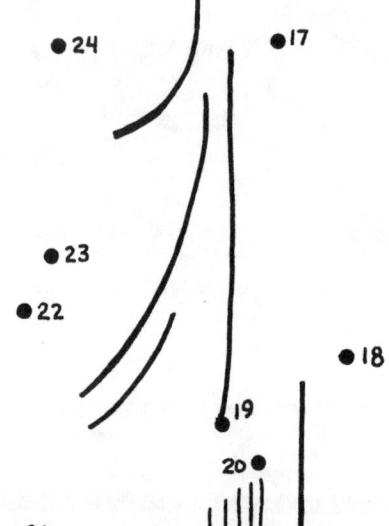

ACTIVITY 2

UNCLE SAM FINGER PUPPET

"TEACHER'S FRIEND" ©   48   JULY & AUGUST

of this classroom have certain individual rights.

I have the right to be happy and to be treated fairly in this room.
No one will make fun of me or hurt my feelings. I will be given the same consideration and respect as others.

I have a right to be safe in this room.
No one will push, hit, kick, pinch or hurt me.

I have a right to hear and be heard in this room.
No one will shout, yell or make loud noises at inappropriate times.

I have a right to learn in this room.
No one will keep me from succeeding in my studies.

I have a right to be myself in this room.
No one will judge me or treat me unfairly because of my color, gender or background.

Visor

Uncle Sam

Enlarge this "Uncle Sam" onto posterboard and display him along the edges of the class bulletin board.

The Great Seal of the United States of America

Creative Writing

Solar System

The sun and all the planets, with their satellites, make up our solar system. The word "solar" comes from the Latin word "sol," meaning sun.

In our solar system there are nine planets. The earth is one of these planets. Six of the planets have moons. The earth has only one moon but the largest planet, Jupiter, has as many as sixteen. Besides the nine planets and moons there are numerous asteroids, meteors and comets.

FACTS ABOUT THE PLANETS

Planet Name	Distance (in miles) from Sun	Diameter in Miles
MERCURY	36,300,000	3,009
VENUS	67,000,000	7,522
EARTH	93,000,000	7,926
MARS	141,400,000	4,196
JUPITER	484,000,000	88,700
SATURN	887,000,000	74,600
URANUS	1,784,000,000	32,500
NEPTUNE	2,796,000,000	30,500
PLUTO	3,668,000,000	1,660

TRY ONE OF THESE ACTIVITIES:

1. Before beginning a new solar system unit, have each of your students write down all that they already know about the subject. Have them list the names of planets, temperatures, distances, sizes and life on other planets. Collect all the information and place it in a sealed envelope. At the completion of the solar system unit, open the envelope and read the numerous misconceptions your students had before.

2. Have each student choose a planet on which to report. Ask them to use their imagination and write about the people that might live there. What type of homes would they need? What would they do for food or water? How would they travel? Ask them to draw a picture of their new planetary settlement.

"TEACHER'S FRIEND" ©   JULY & AUGUST

Space Fun

Unscramble these planet names.

ACTIVITY 3

htaer _ _ _ _ _
uns _ _ _
toupl _ _ _ _ _
neutpne _ _ _ _ _ _ _
suevn _ _ _ _ _
urcyerm _ _ _ _ _ _ _
nusaru _ _ _ _ _ _
rnutsa _ _ _ _ _ _
piertuj _ _ _ _ _ _ _
rasm _ _ _ _

ACTIVITY 4

FIND THESE SPACE WORDS:

ASTRONOMY
ORBIT
TELESCOPE
PLANETS
COMET
ASTEROID
STAR
METEOR
MOON
SATELLITE
ASTRONAUT
SHUTTLE

```
S W E R D S H U T T L E D R E W Q G H Y T
D O D C V F G T R E W S C B G Y T U I P O
S R H Y A S T R O N A U T D E R C Y T H U
C B Y H U J I Y N M H Y T R F R O D R E T
D I S A T E L L I T E D R E R F M G T Y U
S T E L E S C O P E F R V S G T E U I P L
A S D F C V B G T R E D A T D E T F E W S
M E T E O R D R E F R G E A F E W Z X V B
O D E R F H T R W F G B H R R D W C V G H
O D R E A S T E R O I D F V B G H Y T N M
N F R E S D G B F T R E W Q A D F R T G H
K L P L A N E T S T G H Y U N M J K I U H
D C V G F T Y H J A S T R O N O M Y V C X
```

Use several of these words to write a short paragraph about our solar system.

_____
_____
_____
_____
_____

Martian Mania

Celebrate the planet Mars by declaring the day "Martian Mania Day."

Ask your students to come dressed in their silliest clothes. They might wear mismatched patterns or sweaters turned inside out.

Have children make these simple Martian antennae. Glue a paper star or planet on the end of each pipe cleaner. Glitter can be added to the stars for a dazzling effect. Clip the antennae to their head by clipping them in place with hair clips.

Serve Moon Cookies, (sugar cookies) and Martian punch, as a treat in the afternoon.

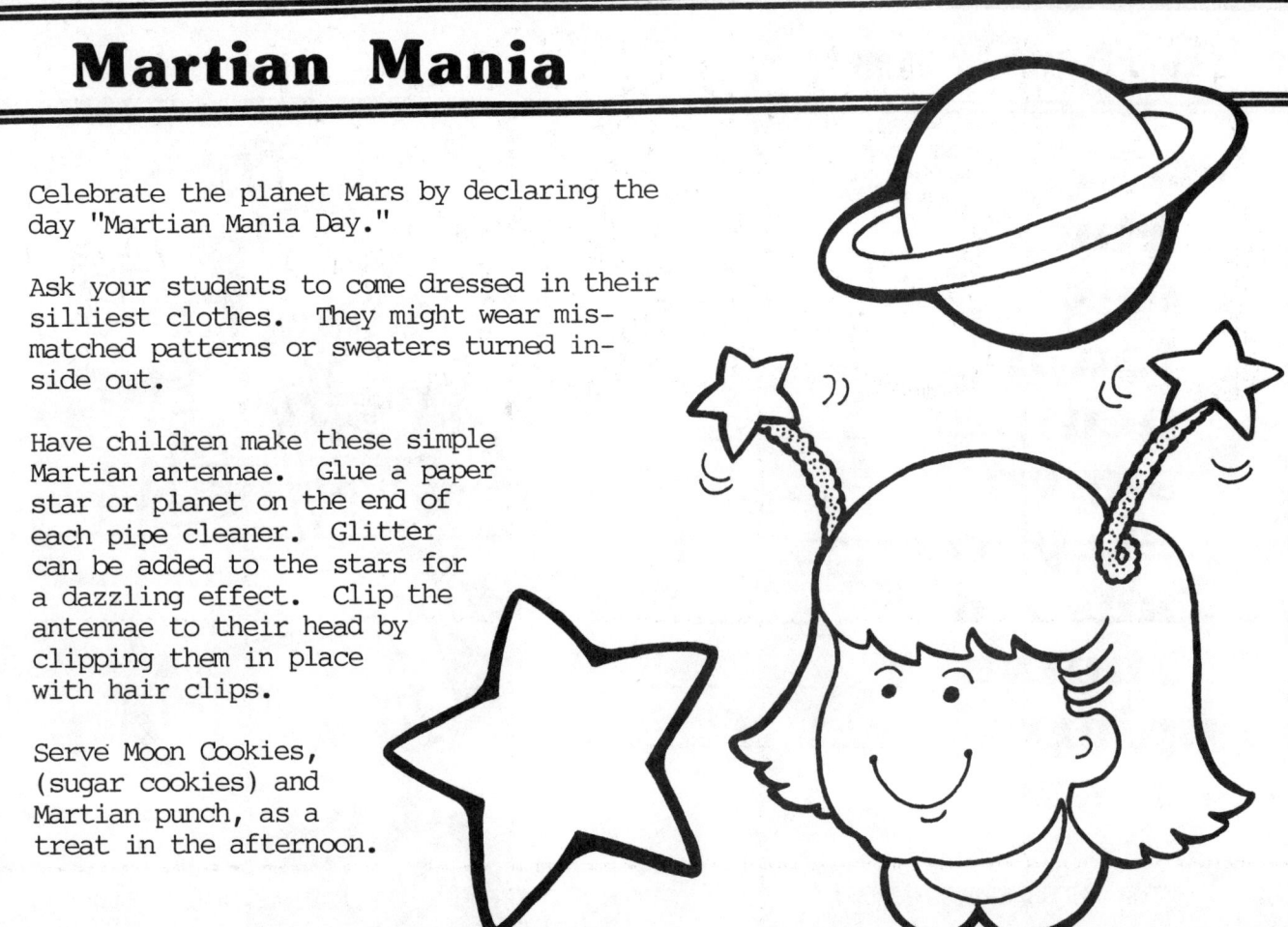

Solar System Bingo

This bingo game offers an exciting way for your students to learn about our solar system. Give each child a copy of the space bingo words listed below or write the words on the class chalkboard. Ask your students to write any 24 words on his or her bingo card. Use the same directions you might use for regular bingo.

SPACE BINGO WORDS

SUN	TELESCOPE	LAUNCH	NASA
MERCURY	PLANETS	PAD	APOLLO
VENUS	COMET	ASTRONAUT	EXPLORER
EARTH	ASTEROID	SHUTTLE	DISCOVERY
MARS	STAR	GRAVITY	CHALLENGER
JUPITER	ASTRONOMY	ATMOSPHERE	OXYGEN
SATURN	METEOR	FLIGHT	GALAXY
URANUS	SATELLITE	VOYAGE	CONSTELLATION
NEPTUNE	SOLAR	COUNTDOWN	NOVA
PLUTO	SYSTEM	UNIVERSE	SPHERE
MOON	SPACE	CREW	AIR
ORBIT	ROCKET	LUNAR	OBSERVATORY

"TEACHER'S FRIEND" ©   JULY & AUGUST

Astronaut Wheel

Copy this "Astronaut" wheel onto heavy index paper. Color, cut out and assemble with brass fasteners. Cut out the two boxes, as shown.

Add your own math problems and answers to the wheel on the next page. Move the flag to reveal the answers.

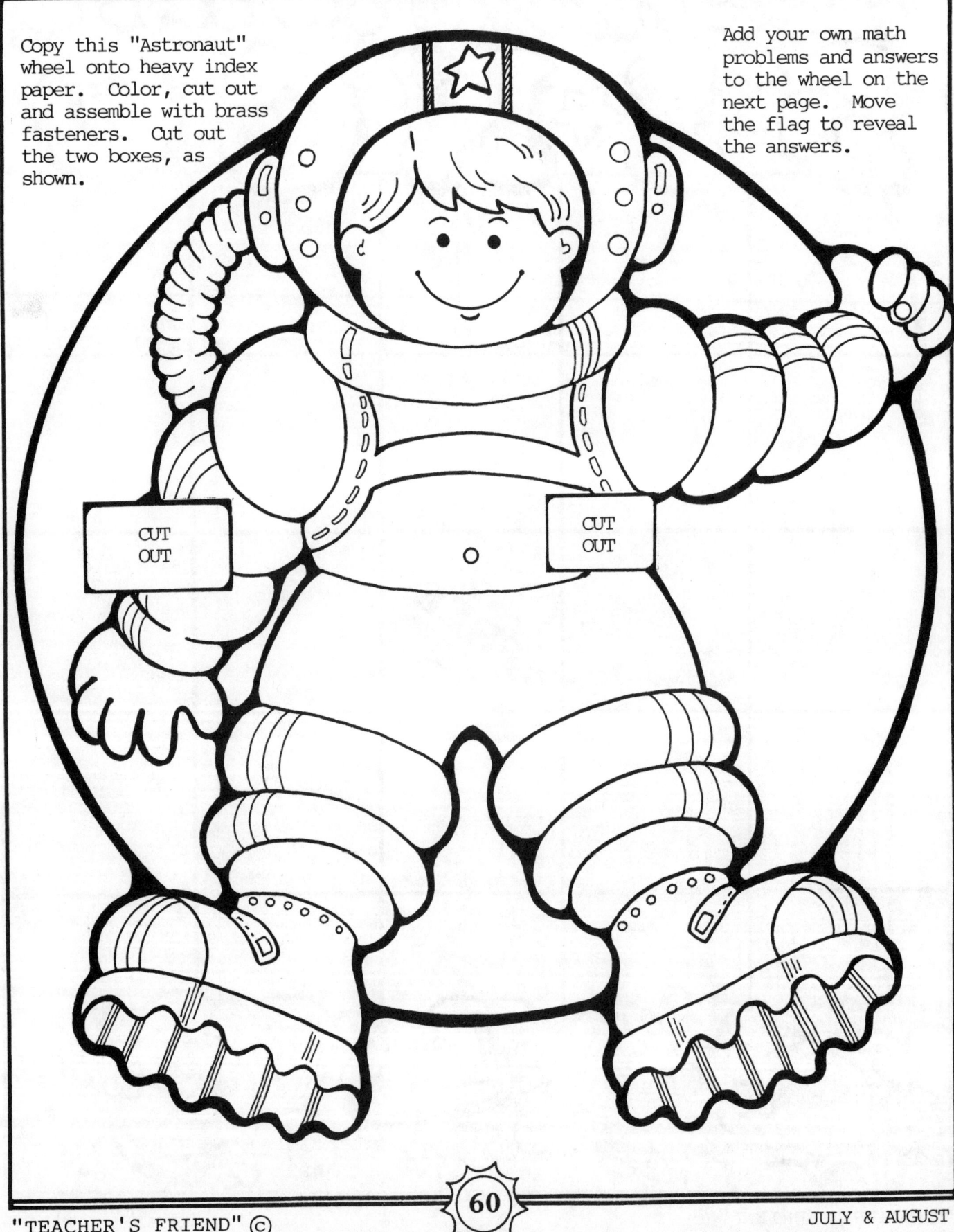

"TEACHER'S FRIEND" ©

JULY & AUGUST

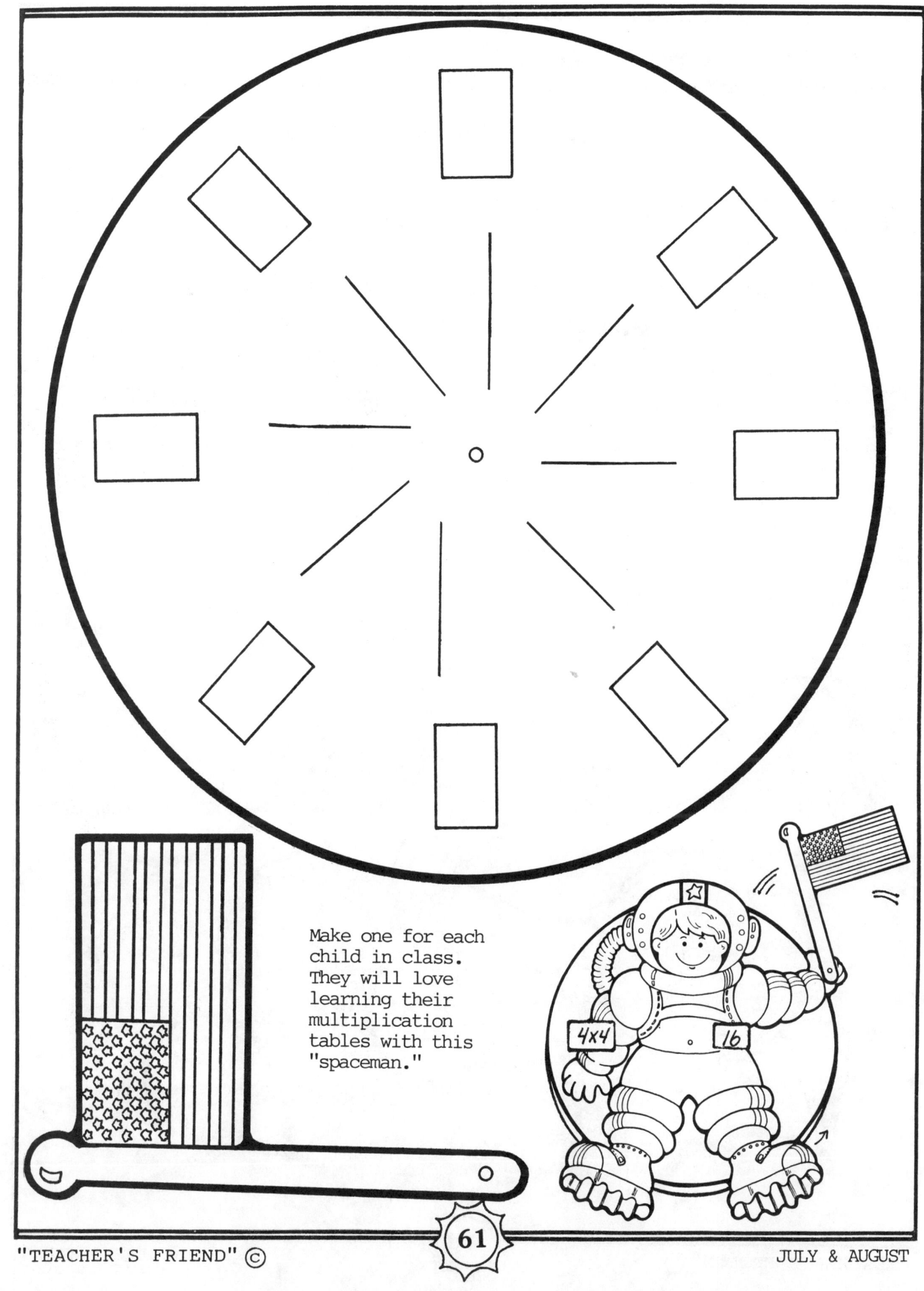

Make one for each child in class. They will love learning their multiplication tables with this "spaceman."

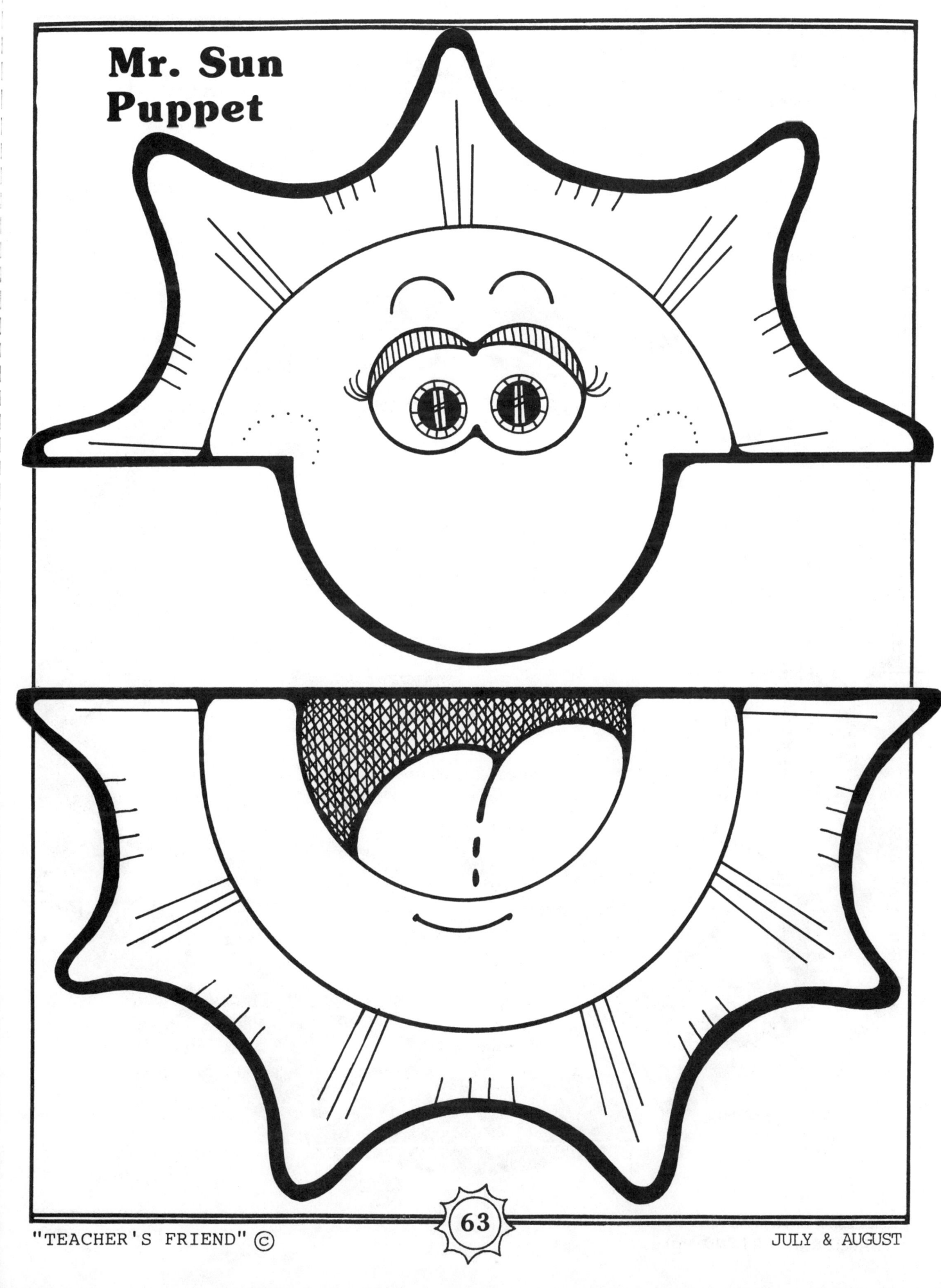

Solar System Mobile

You can make a variety of different mobiles with these planet patterns. Each child might wish to make their own, or you could simply arrange the planets on the class bulletin board.

THE SUN

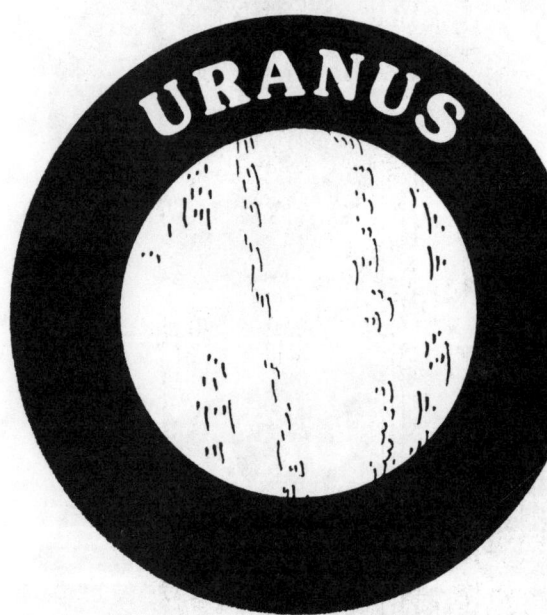

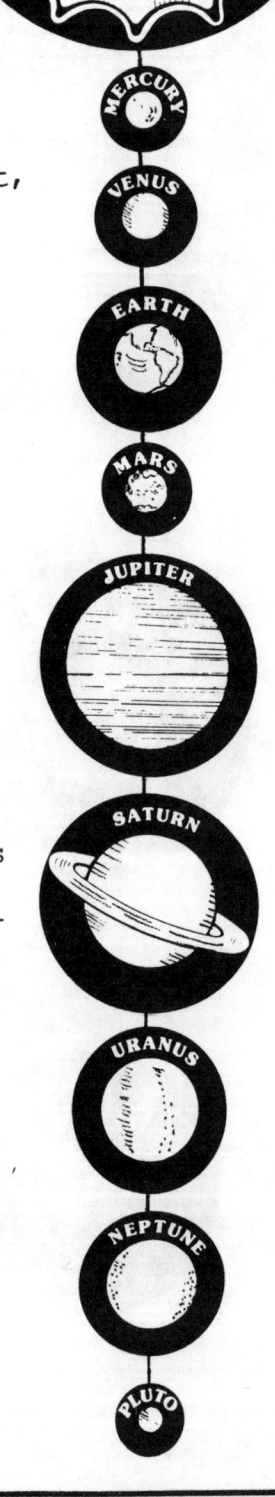

Make two copies of each planet and sun pattern and color with crayons. Cut out each pattern piece. Glue each planet, (back to back) down a long piece of string or yarn. Position the planets in the order of their orbit around the sun. Hang the mobile from the class ceiling, or have each child make their own mobile and hang it in their room.

This planet mobile can also be arranged horizontally. Attach the planets along a piece of yarn, as described above. The display will reach from one side of your classroom to the other if you space the planets apart according to scale.

Star Puzzle

Make several copies of this star pattern on index or construction paper. Write your own math problems on each star point, as shown. Write the answers on the center of the star. Cut all five points of the star off and place the star pieces in an envelope. Have the individual student take the envelope to his or her desk and assemble the star, answering the problems correctly. This is a great way to practice multiplication facts.

A starry bulletin board can be created by asking the children to pin the completed star puzzles to the classroom board. Add a rocket ship or spaceman character to the board.

SPACE Award

This award is presented to

_____

for the completion of the space unit.

Job well done!

_____ _____
date   signature

Award each child this "Space Badge" when they have completed the space unit.

SPACE BADGE

Name _____

The badge can also be used to form space patrols. Each patrol's spaceship should be a different color. The patrols, or teams, can be given separate classroom duties or play as teams for a space spelling bee, or rocket relay games.

Nutrition

- SUMMER RECIPES
- BASIC FOOD GROUPS
- FOOD GROUP CARD GAME
- RECIPE CARDS
- CANDY BAR
- HAMBURGER MOBILE
- BUNCH OF GRAPES PUPPET
- PIZZA AWARD
- FOOD GROUP CHARACTERS
- MY WEEKLY DIET

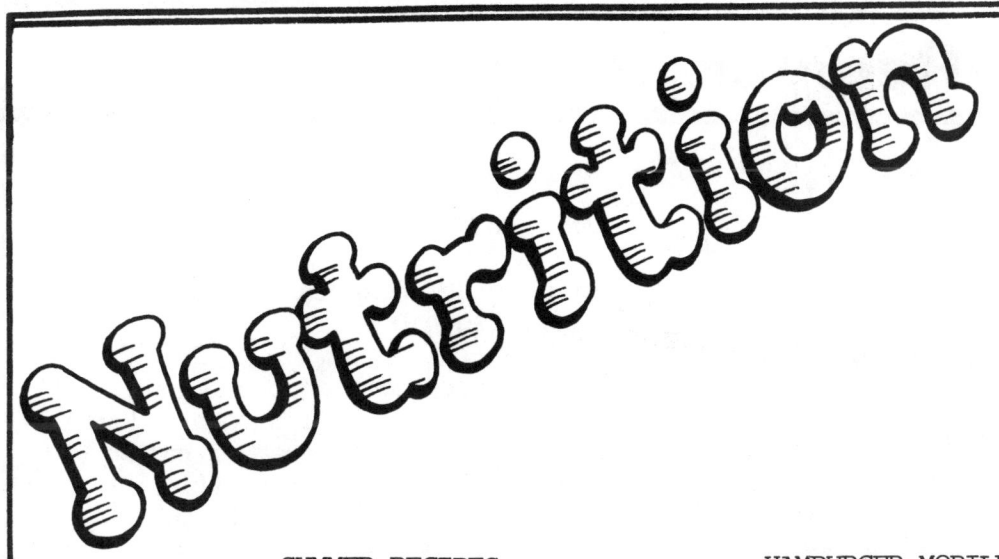

Summer Recipes

CARROT SALAD

1 carrot
4 tsp. raisins
2 Tbsp. mayonnaise
4 tsp. chopped nuts

Carefully grate the carrot into a small mixing bowl. Add the other ingredients and stir together. Refrigerate or eat immediately.

PEANUT BUTTER

1 cup roasted peanuts
2 Tbsp. vegetable oil

In a blender, combine the peanuts and oil and blend til smooth. You might want to add a dash of salt for flavor. Stuff celery sticks or slices of apple with the peanut butter for a refreshing summertime treat.

FUZZY BANANAS

1 pint sour cream or yogurt
1 banana for every four children
1 package shredded coconut
1 box of toothpicks

Spear the banana chunks with a toothpick and dip into the yogurt, coating it thoroughly. Roll it in the coconut and eat right away.

NUTRITIOUS CANDY

1 cup peanut butter
1/2 cup honey
1/4 cup sunflower seeds
1/4 cup wheat germ
1/4 cup dried skim milk
2 tsp. vanilla
crushed corn flakes or
    shredded coconut

Mix the first six ingredients together and shape into small balls. Roll the balls into the coconut or corn flakes. Refrigerate before eating. Makes about 40 small balls.

SUMMER PARFAITS

Parfaits are made with a variety of layered ingredients. Give each student a clear plastic cup and have them select four or five items from the list below and create their own super summer parfait!

pudding	jello	jelly beans
whipped cream	marshmallows	banana slices
yogurt	coconut	dry cereal
sherbet	raisins	chocolate chips
ice cream	nuts	sunflower seeds
canned fruit	applesauce	strawberries

"TEACHER'S FRIEND" ©   JULY & AUGUST

Four Basic Food Groups

Milk Group

Bread & Cereal Group

Meat Group

Fruit & Vegetable Group

Food Group Card Game

Students will be motivated to learn more about the four basic food groups and the food that they contain with these simple card games.

FOOD GROUPS CONCENTRATION

Two students play the game by shuffling the cards and laying them face down on a table top. Each player takes turns revealing three cards at a time, trying to match the food group. If the cards match, the player keeps the cards and draws again until the cards do not match. Cards that do not match are returned to their exact spot and the player forfeits his or her turn to the other player. The game continues until all cards are matched. The player with the most cards, wins the game.

GO FISH FOOD GROUPS

Three or four students can play this game. Make four copies of each card and have each player draw five cards. Place the remaining cards in a stack in the middle of the table. An example of play might be: player #1 asks player #2 if he or she has an "ice cream card." If player #2 has the card, he or she must give it to the first player. When player #1 collects four ice cream cards, the cards are placed face down on the table and points counted. If player #2 does not have the card, the first player must "fish" a card from the center stack. The game continues until all cards are matched. The player with the most points or matched sets, wins the game.

FRUIT & VEGETABLE GROUP 	 FRUIT & VEGETABLE GROUP
 FRUIT & VEGETABLE GROUP	BREAD & CEREAL GROUP 

"TEACHER'S FRIEND" ©   JULY & AUGUST

Food Group Card Game

MILK GROUP

MILK GROUP

MILK GROUP

MEAT GROUP

MEAT GROUP

MEAT GROUP

BREAD & CEREAL GROUP

BREAD & CEREAL GROUP

"TEACHER'S FRIEND" ©

JULY & AUGUST

Important Nutrients

List foods that contain these important nutrients.

Vitamin A increases resistance to infection and improves eyesight.

Vitamin B aids in good digestion and steady nerves.

Vitamin C prevents scurvy and helps our muscles and gums.

Vitamin D helps keep our teeth and bones healthy and strong.

Carbohydrates give us strength and energy.

Fats, in correct amounts, enhances our skin and gives us energy.

Proteins build and repair our bodies.

Recipe Cards

Name of Recipe
Ingredients:

Directions:

Name of Recipe
Ingredients:

Directions:

Nutritious Candy Bar

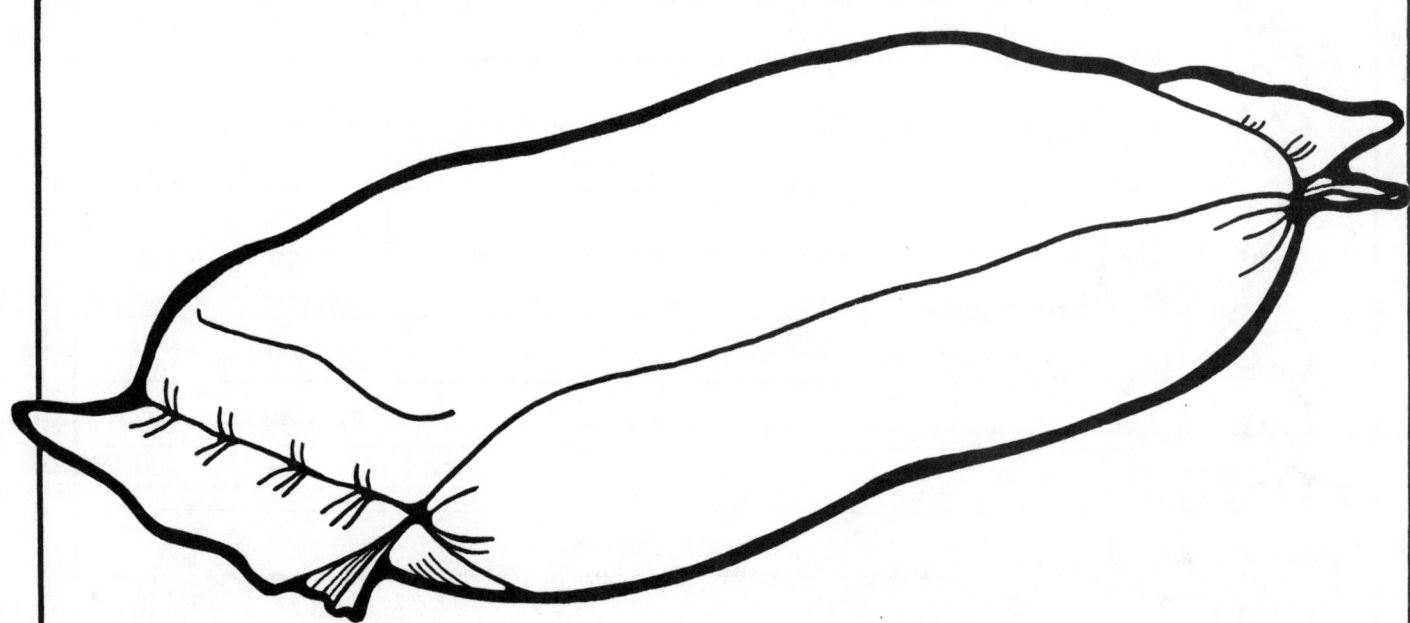

Create a nutritious candy bar that will not only be good to eat but also good for you!

List your special ingredients and then select a name for your new candy bar. You might want to write a slogan that can be used to advertise it. Lastly, design a new wrapper for your candy bar creation.

Ingredients: _____

_____

_____

_____

_____

Name: _____

_____

Slogan: _____

_____

_____

_____

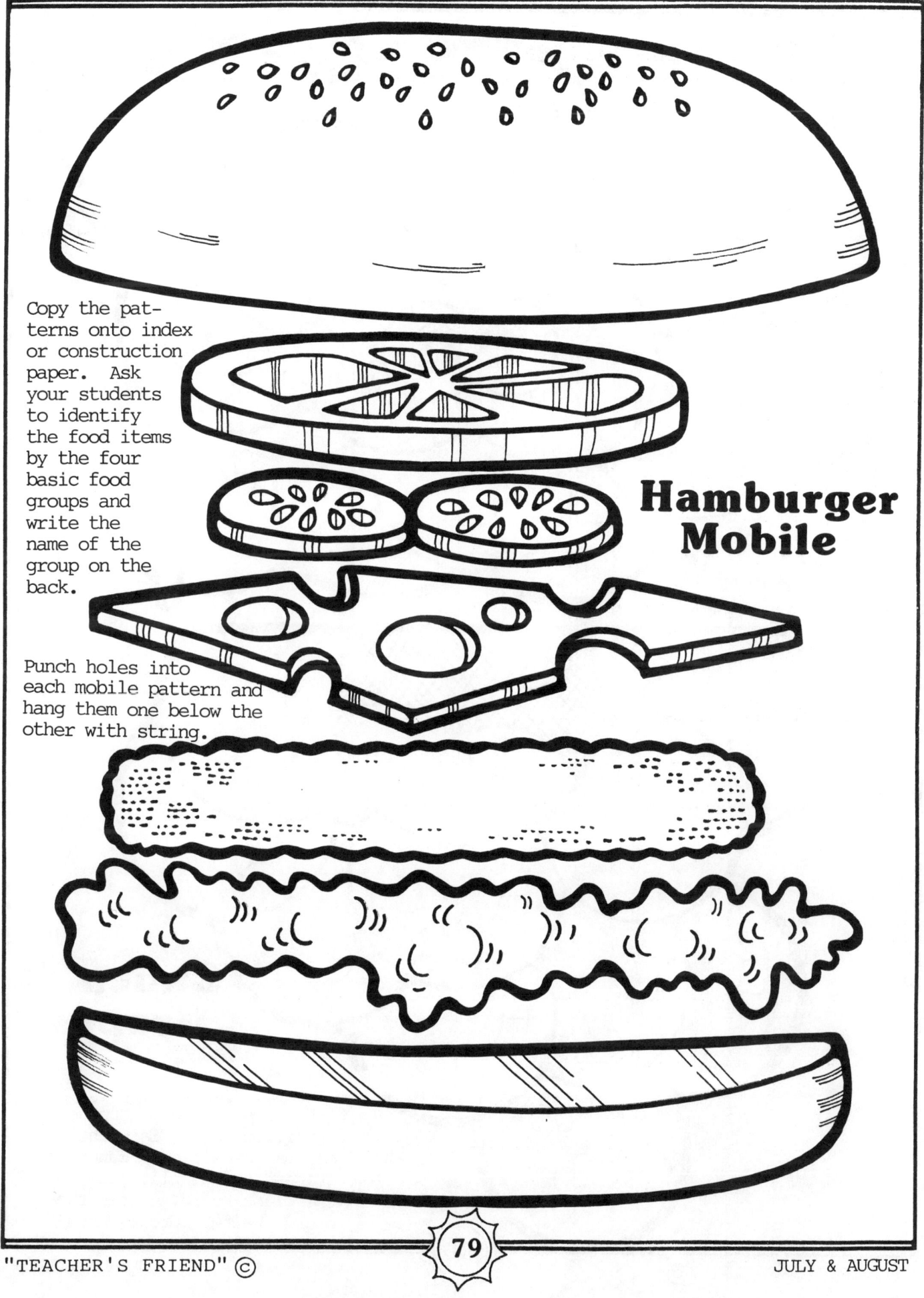

Copy the patterns onto index or construction paper. Ask your students to identify the food items by the four basic food groups and write the name of the group on the back.

Punch holes into each mobile pattern and hang them one below the other with string.

Hamburger Mobile

"TEACHER'S FRIEND" ©   JULY & AUGUST

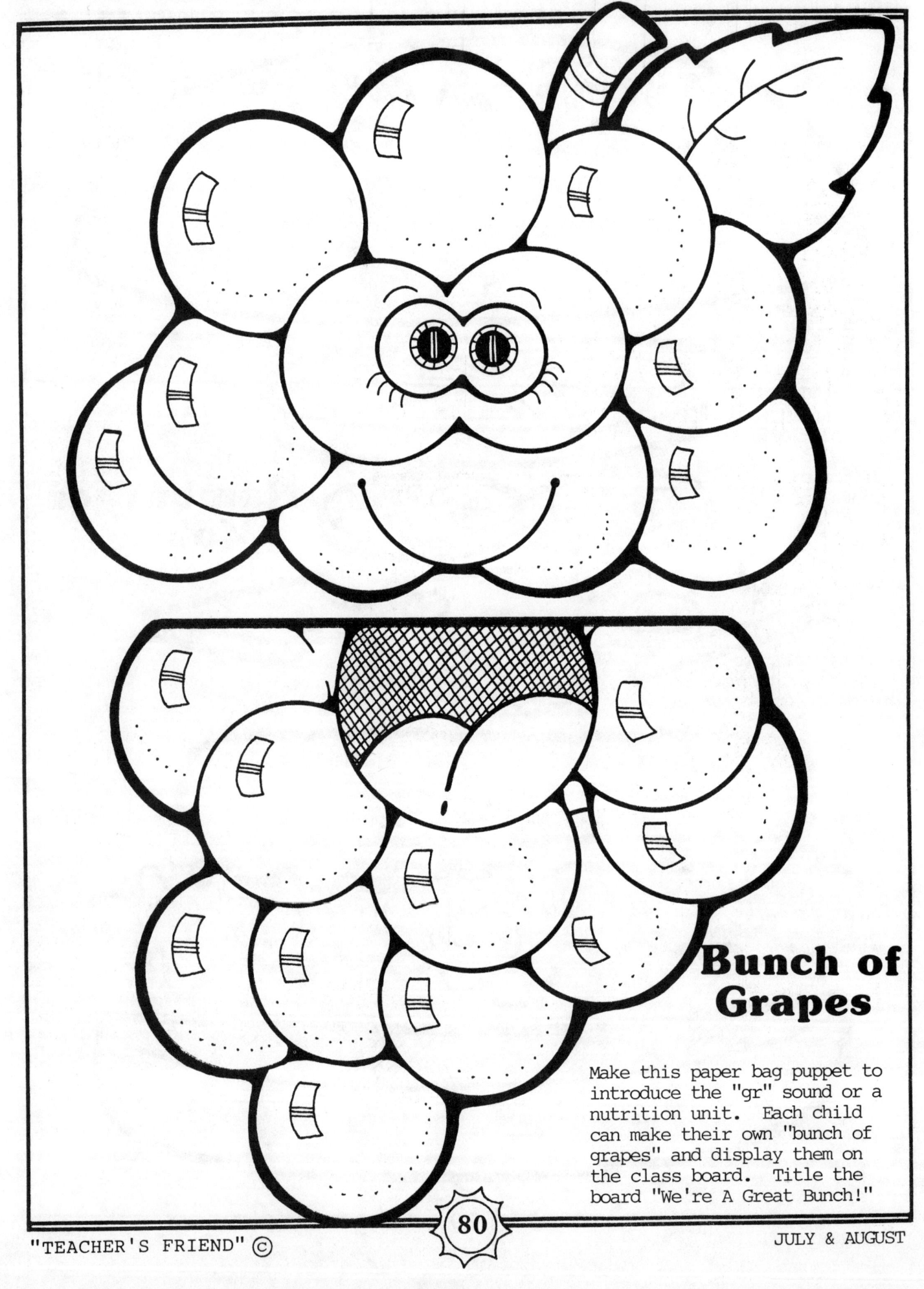

Bunch of Grapes

Make this paper bag puppet to introduce the "gr" sound or a nutrition unit. Each child can make their own "bunch of grapes" and display them on the class board. Title the board "We're A Great Bunch!"

Pizza Award

The next time you wish to award your students with an extra special treat, give them a piece of pizza!

As each student receives their piece of pizza, display them on the class bulletin board, as illustrated. You might want each student to collect six pieces of pizza.

Throw a real pizza party for your class when all the students have earned their pizza award!

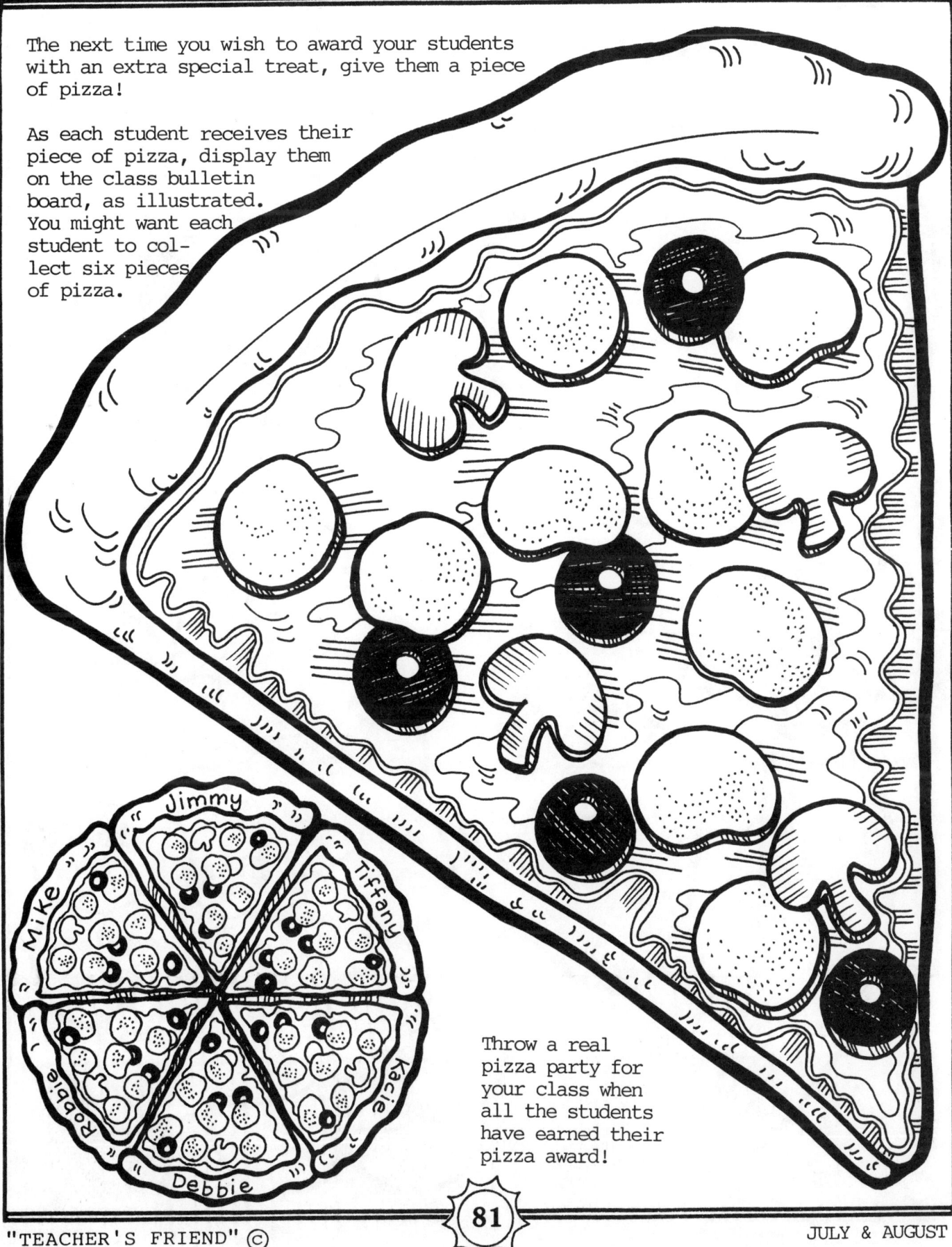

"TEACHER'S FRIEND" ©

JULY & AUGUST

Food Group Characters

My Weekly Diet

	MON.	TUE.	WED.	THUR.	FRI.
BREAKFAST					
LUNCH					
DINNER					

"TEACHER'S FRIEND" ©   JULY & AUGUST

Travel & Transportation

- TRAVEL ACTIVITIES
- TRAVEL BINGO
- MY TRIP RECORD
- TRAVEL STORY STARTERS
- SCHOOL BUS RULES

Travel Activities

DESIGN A POSTCARD

Ask your students to pick a well known local landmark and design a colorful postcard. They can use markers, crayons or colored pencils. When their creation is finished, ask them to write a message to a friend or relative on the back and mail it through the U.S. post office.

MAPS, MAPS, MAPS

Start a classroom map collection. Ask your students to find as many different maps as possible and bring them to class. Post the maps on the class bulletin board and develop a variety of math and research questions that can be done during free time.

Here are some suggestions:

roap maps
subway maps
geological maps
weather maps
oceanography maps
moon maps
population maps
bus route maps

SCHOOL BOUND

Ask your students to observe what they see and hear on their way to school. Ask them to note the different types of transportation they see. Have them count the number of streets they cross or how many right or left turns they make. Do they see people or animals on their journey to school?

At the conclusion of the exercise, have the students each draw a detailed map of their route to school. Ask them to include buildings, people, dogs, trees and stop signs.

Travel Bingo

This travel bingo game offers an interesting way to keep students occupied during the next field trip or family vacation. Before the trip, give each child a copy of the blank bingo card. Have them write the names of the various things they might see during the trip, on the card. During the travel portion of the trip, when a child sees an item on their card, they cross it out. (You might want them to shout out the item when it is spotted.) The first student to cross out five squares in a row, wins the game.

Some items for suggestion:

police car
motorcycle
pickup truck
dump truck
travel trailer
motorhome

out of state license
fire truck
stop sign
billboard
red barn
milk truck

railroad crossing
skyscraper
bridge
tunnel
lake
river

Transportation Fun

ACTIVITY 5

FIND THESE TRANSPORTATION WORDS:

- boat
- airplane
- monorail
- motorcycle
- bicycle
- train
- bus
- submarine
- balloon
- helicopter
- walking
- ship
- tram
- skateboard
- horse
- truck
- taxi
- car

```
A C X D S W E B I C Y C L E S C V B G T
A X D F C V G U W E R G B N M J K L I O
B A L L O O N S W F B N H J U Y T R E W
O X C V B N M J K S K A T E B O A R D Q
A S D R E F G H Y H O R S E C V F G T Y
T C V B G F D E W I D F V B G H N J U Y
A I R P L A N E R P C F T R A I N V B H
X C V B G H N M J C D E W R T U I O P J
I F G H J K L M N A G T T R E W Q B G H
C F N M O C T Y H R C V B N J H T R A M
C V M O N O R A I L D F R E W Q R T H T
B F R T G H Y U J K I L O P M N H G F R
A S S U B M A R I N E D E R T G H Y U U
C W V G H F G T M O T O R C Y C L E D C
V B N H S Q T Y F N H Y U J K L O P V K
H E L I C O P T E R C V F G T H B N J U
C V B G F D E W A L K I N G C F D R T Y
```

ACTIVITY 6

terpoclihe _ _ _ _ _ _ _ _ _ _

aubilemoto _ _ _ _ _ _ _ _ _ _

llbanoo _ _ _ _ _ _ _

riaplnea _ _ _ _ _ _ _ _

teskabrdoa _ _ _ _ _ _ _ _ _ _

taobails _ _ _ _ _ _ _ _

cleycbi _ _ _ _ _ _ _

ketcor _ _ _ _ _ _

Unscramble these transportation words: rocket, bicycle, sailboat, skateboard, automobile, airplane, helicopter and balloon

"TEACHER'S FRIEND" ©   JULY & AUGUST

My Trip Record

Where I went: _____
_____
_____

Dates: _____
_____

Travel time: _____
_____

Type of transportation: _____
_____

People I traveled with: _____
_____

People I met: _____
_____

Places I visited: _____
_____
_____

What I enjoyed most: _____
_____
_____
_____
_____

What I enjoyed least: _____
_____
_____
_____

Traveling Story Starters

Suddenly, a car traveling 120 mph passed me on the highway!

There I was, in the middle of nowhere, when the car ran out of gas!

The used car salesman said it was a very "special" car!

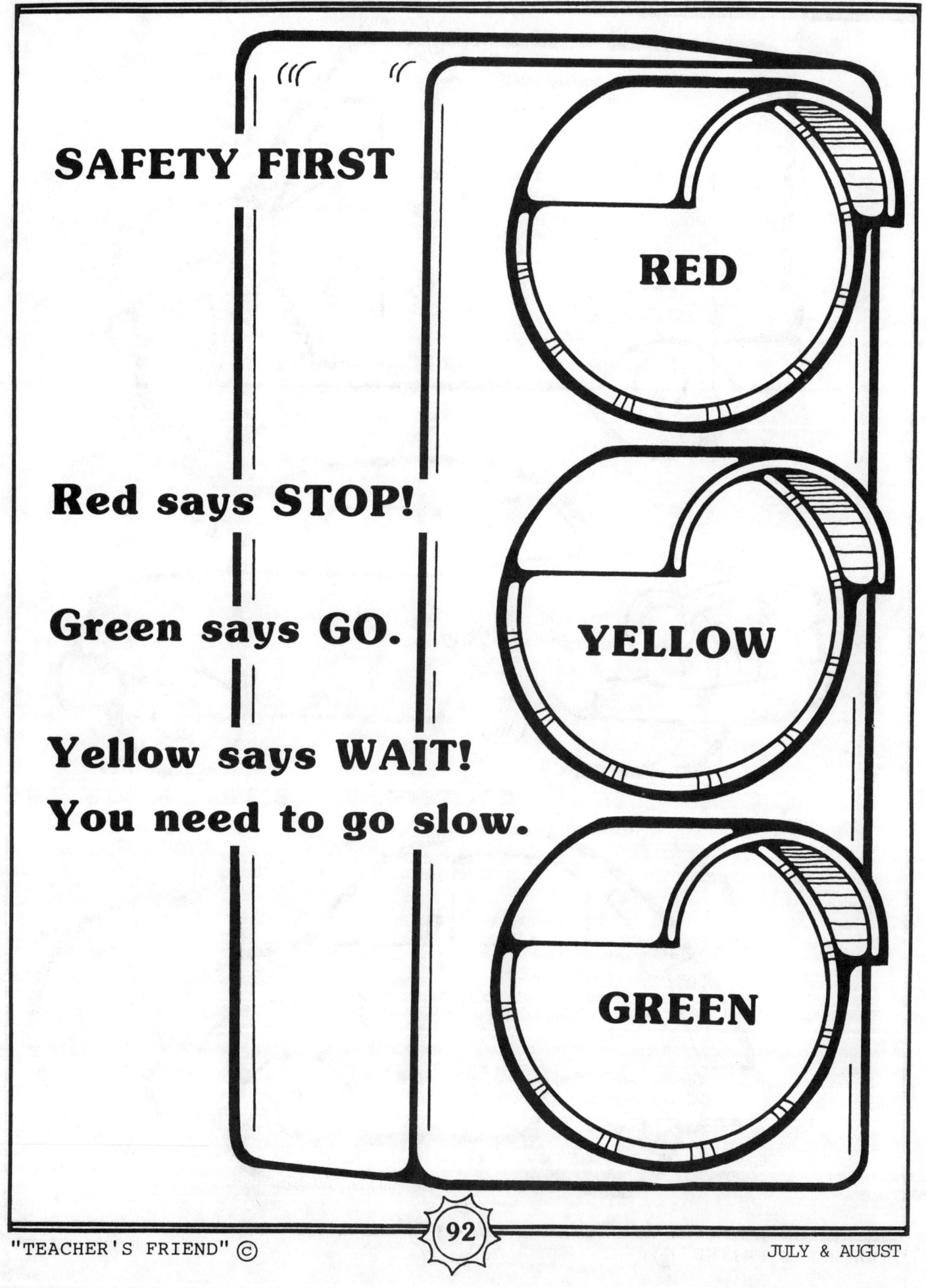

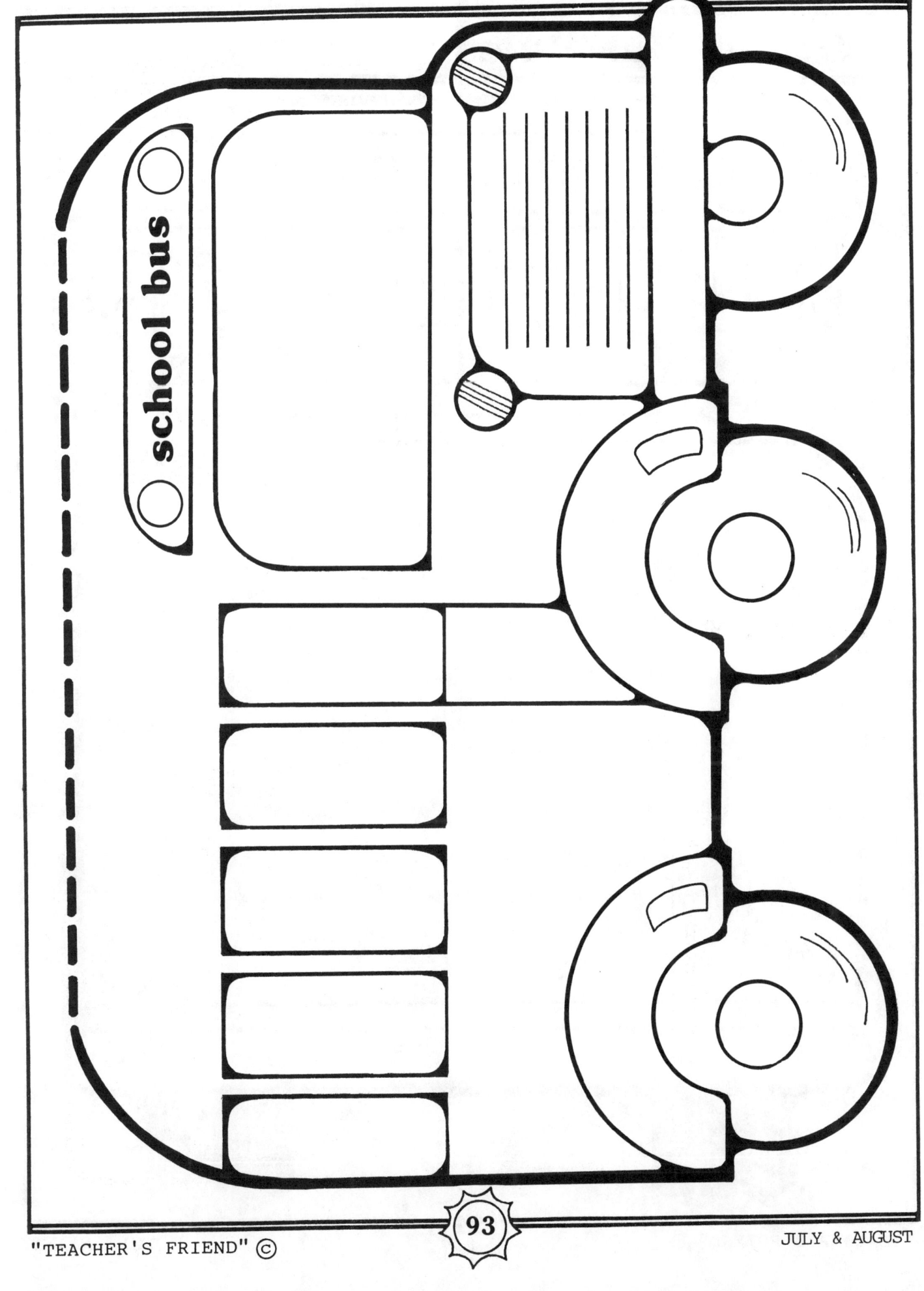

School Bus Rules

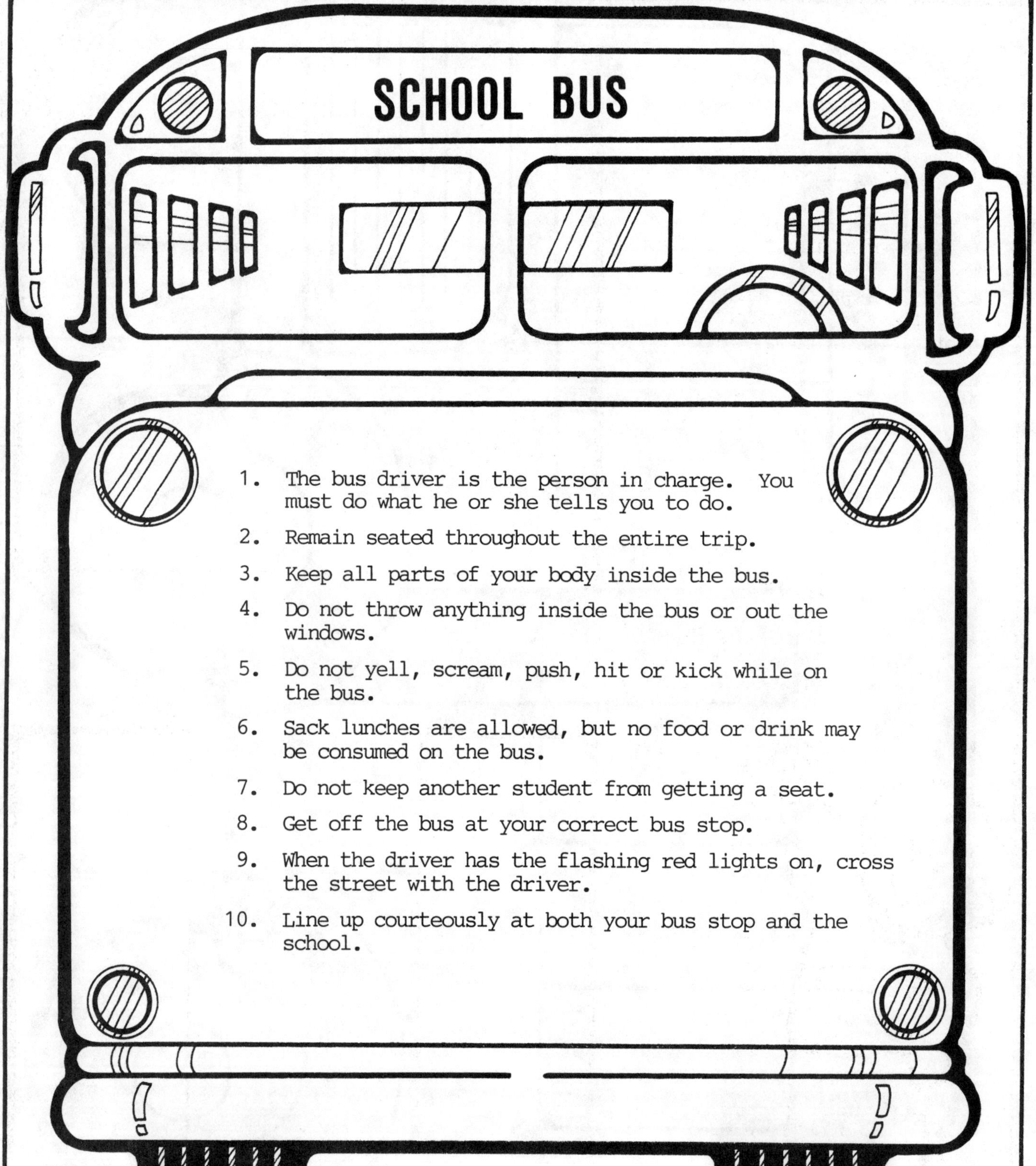

SCHOOL BUS

1. The bus driver is the person in charge. You must do what he or she tells you to do.
2. Remain seated throughout the entire trip.
3. Keep all parts of your body inside the bus.
4. Do not throw anything inside the bus or out the windows.
5. Do not yell, scream, push, hit or kick while on the bus.
6. Sack lunches are allowed, but no food or drink may be consumed on the bus.
7. Do not keep another student from getting a seat.
8. Get off the bus at your correct bus stop.
9. When the driver has the flashing red lights on, cross the street with the driver.
10. Line up courteously at both your bus stop and the school.

Spiral Helicopter

Copy this pattern onto construction paper and cut it out. Fold along the dotted lines, making sure to fold the blades of the helicopter in opposite directions.

Attach a paper clip to the bottom portion of the helicopter. Now, you're ready to fly! Toss the helicopter into the air and watch it gently spiral to the ground.

"TEACHER'S FRIEND" ©

JULY & AUGUST

Creative Writing

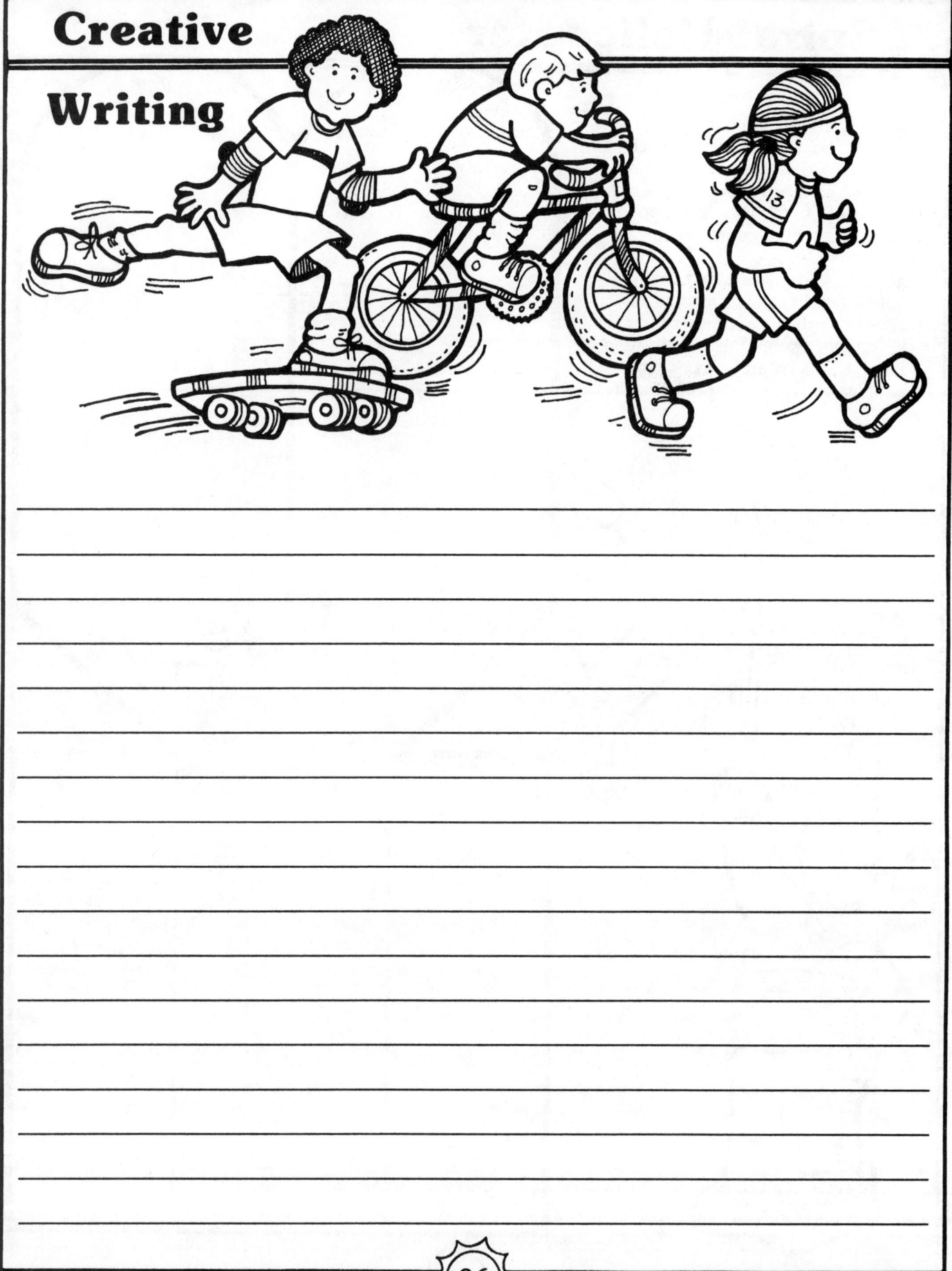

Bulletin Boards

FLYING HIGH - Use a real kite for this cute bulletin board or make your own. Make a tail with twisted crepe paper. Cut paper bows and label each one with a student's name. This is a great way to welcome kids to class!

SUMMERTIME HAPPENINGS - Display a large yellow sun in the center of the class bulletin board. Give each student a white paper cloud and ask them to write about their favorite summertime experience. Arrange the clouds around the sun for a bright and cheery display.

CHOOSE WELL - Encourage your students to wisely choose the types of foods they eat with this simple bulletin board. The students can cut food pictures from magazines or draw their own nutritious goodies.

"TEACHER'S FRIEND" ©   JULY & AUGUST

and more...

SCHOOL BUS RULES - Display a large yellow school bus on the class bulletin board. List different rules of bus safety on strips of paper and arrange them around the bus. Children might like to draw portraits of themselves that can be placed in the bus windows.

TELEPHONE NUMBERS - Teach your students important numbers along with their home phone numbers with this simple bulletin board. As each child memorizes their phone number, they can write it on a strip of paper along with their name and display it on the board around a large paper telephone. Also, encourage them to memorize emergency numbers.

SHOOTING STARS - Make everyone in class a super star with this idea. Each child can earn their own star, to place on the board, when a certain task is accomplished. This is a great way to show off good work papers.

and more!

WE'RE REALLY COOKING! - Let your students display creative recipes with this easy bulletin board. Cut a large French chef from colored paper and place him on one side of the board. Students can write their recipes on recipe cards and display them around the the chef.

LET FREEDOM RING! - Celebrate the Fourth of July with a display of the Liberty Bell.

Children's research papers or thoughts about freedom can be displayed on the board.

A GREAT BUNCH! - Cut large circles from purple construction paper for this simple board. Arrange them, as shown, and write each student's name on a grape. Children love to see their name in print and this bulletin board is a perfect way to do just that!

"TEACHER'S FRIEND" ©   JULY & AUGUST

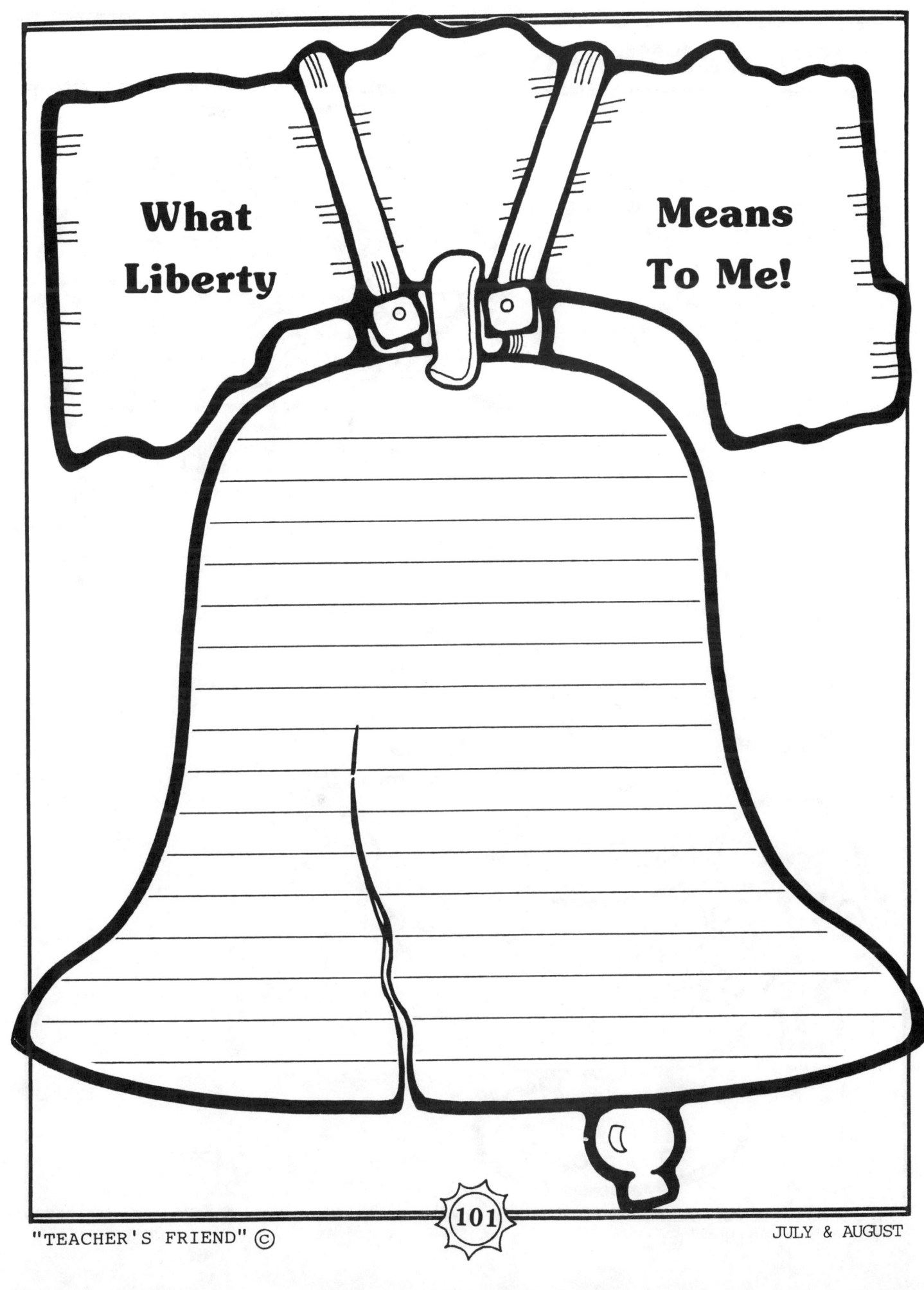

Wishful Thinking

Use these "wishful" symbols to motivate your students with creative writing assignments.

Enlarge the magic lamp or the wishing well on the class bulletin board and have students write about their favorite dream or wish.

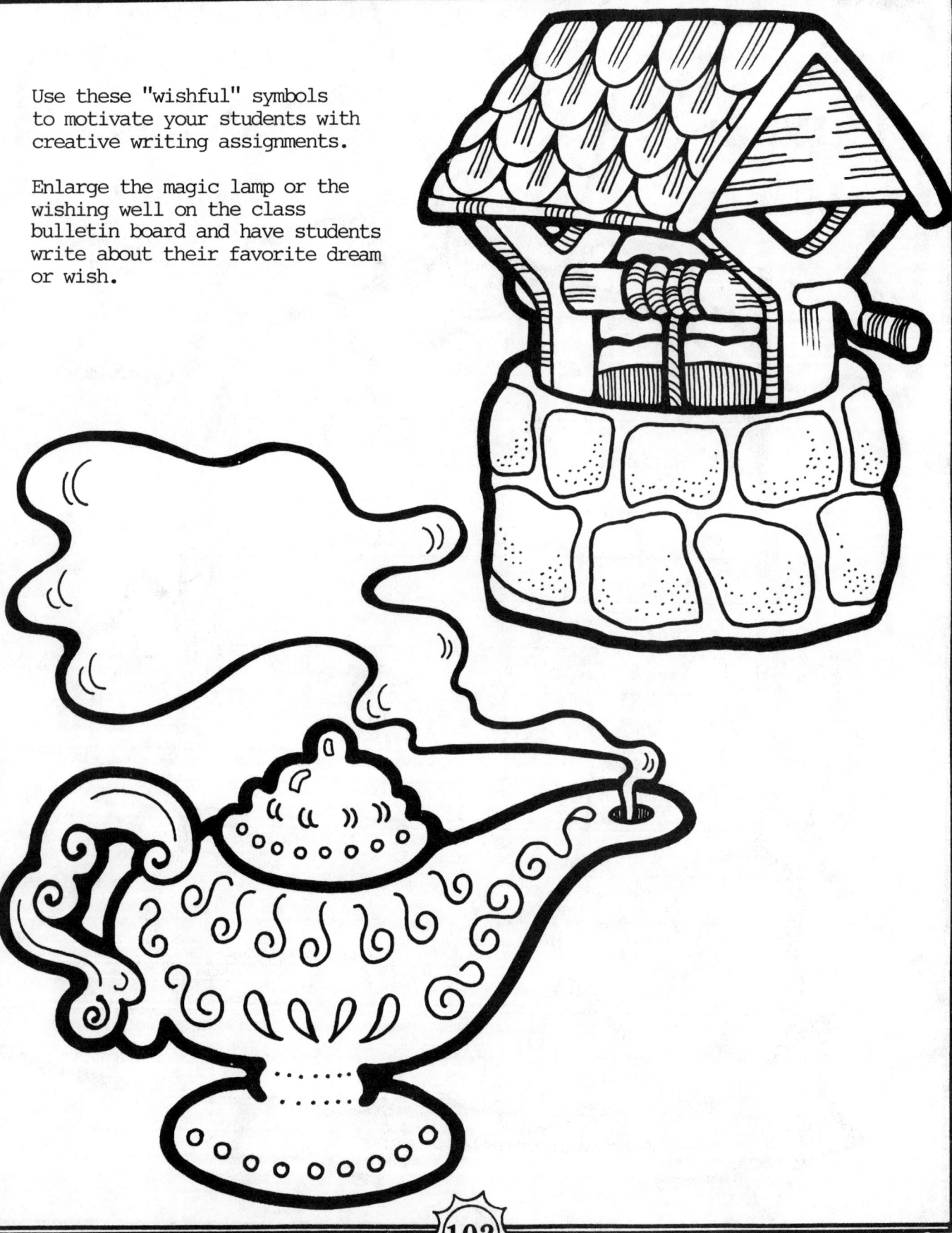

"TEACHER'S FRIEND" ©

JULY & AUGUST

Answer Key

FIND THESE PATRIOTIC WORDS:

INDEPENDENCE
DECLARATION
LIBERTY
JUSTICE
PATRIOTISM
STARS
STRIPES
UNCLE SAM
FLAG
GLORY
AMERICA
FREEDOM

```
X C F T R E V F R E E D O M D F T Y U N H
D F L D T Y G H J U S E T E O U L K J H R
F Y A R G T Y J U S T I C E D E W R T Y U
W Q G F G T Y H J U I K L O P H J S R T Y
  P A T R I O T I S M S W Q E R T Y T V B N
S D F R T G G D E D S E W D S W T A Y U I
F B V C X L T Y U I L I B E R T Y R E W Q
D C V F G O G T H D E S E S A E T S T U Y
F B V C X R F A M E R I C A D R E T G T U
C V B F G Y D R E F G T H Y U J K R F T R
  U N C L E S A M D R F G T Y H J U I D F R
A S D F R E G V B N M J H K I U J P D V B
F G D E C L A R A T I O N D F R T E R G H
D F V G B H N J M K L O I K J M N S F R T
D V B G F B N G G I N D E P E N D E N C E
S C V B H G N M J K L O I K M J N H Y T G
```

ACTIVITY 1

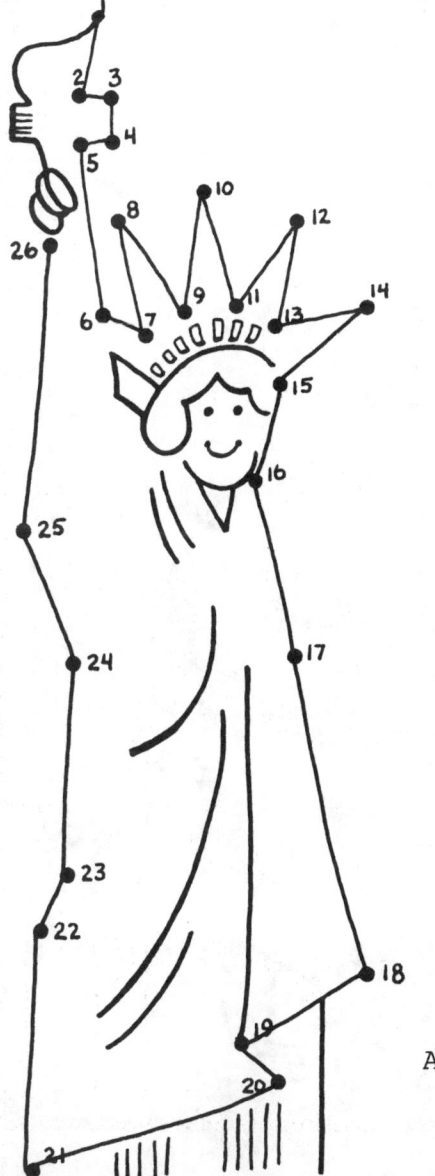

ACTIVITY 2

Unscramble these planet names.

htaer earth
uns sun
toupl pluto
neutpne neptune
suevn venus
urcyerm mercury
nusaru uranus
rnutsa saturn
piertuj jupiter
rasm mars

ACTIVITY 3

Answer Key

ACTIVITY 4

```
S W E R D S H U T T L E D R E W Q G H Y T
D O D C V F G T R E W S C B G Y T U I P O
S R H Y A S T R O N A U T D E R C Y T H U
C B Y H U J I Y N M H Y T R F O D R E T
D I S A T E L L I T E D R E R F M G T Y U
S T E L E S C O P E F R V S G T E U I P L
A S D F C V B G T R E D A T D E T F E W S
M E T E O R D R E F R G E A F E W Z X V B
O D E R F H T R W F G B H R R D W C V G H
O D R E A S T E R O I D F V B G H Y T N M
N F R E S D G B F T R E W Q A D F R T G H
K L P L A N E T S T G H Y U N M J K I U H
D C V G F T Y H J A S T R O N O M Y V C X
```

ACTIVITY 5

```
A C X D S W E B I C Y C L E S C V B G T
A X D F C V G U W E R G B N M J K L I O
B A L L O O N S W F B N H J U Y T R E W
O X C V B N M J K S K A T E B O A R D Q
A S D R E F G H Y H O R S E C V F G T Y
T C V B G F D E W I D F V B G H N J U Y
A I R P L A N E R P C F T R A I N V B H
X C V B G H N M J C D E W R T U I O P J
I F G H J K L M N A G T T R E W Q B G H
C F N M O C T Y H R C V B N J W T R A M
C V M C N O R A I L D F R E W Q R T H T
B F R T G H Y U J K I L O P M N H G F R
A S S U B M A R I N E D E R T G H Y U U
C W V G H F G T M O T O R C Y C L E D C
V B N H S Q T Y F N H Y U J K L O P V K
H E L I C O P T E R C V F G T H B N J U
C V B G F D E W A L K I N G C F D R T Y
```

ACTIVITY 6

terpoclihe helicopter
aubilemoto automobile
llbanoo balloon
riaplnea airplane
teskabrdoa skateboard
taobails sailboat
cleycbi bicycle
ketcor rocket

"TEACHER'S FRIEND" ©   JULY & AUGUST

Index To All Teacher's Friend Idea Books

A
AMERICAN INDIAN ACTIVITIES
September pp 89-96
November pp 33-50

AMPHIBIANS
March pp 102
June pp 63-82

APPLE ACTIVITIES
September pp 73-80

AUTUMN ACTIVITIES
October pp 19-32
November pp 28-32

B
BACK TO SCHOOL ACTIVITIES
September pp 25-36
July & Aug. pp 34-44
103-108

BEES
April pp 64-73

BIRD WATCHING
May pp 63-82

BIRTHDAYS
September pp 71, 105

BUGS (INSECTS)
April pp 50-54

BUTTERFLIES
April pp 56-63

C
CHILDREN'S BOOK WEEK
November pp 61-72

CHINESE NEW YEAR
January pp 57-70

CHRISTMAS ACTIVITIES
December pp 19-66

CHRISTMAS (INTERNATIONAL)
MEXICO - December pp 67-72
ITALY - December pp 73-78
HOLLAND - December pp 79-86
SWEDEN - December pp 87-92

CINCO DE MAYO
May pp 53-62

CIRCUS ACTIVITIES
May pp 83-98

CLASSROOM HELPERS
September pp 107
November pp 105

COLUMBUS DAY
October pp 67-74

D
DENTAL HEALTH
February pp 73-82

DINOSAURS
October pp 33-44

E
EASTER ACTIVITIES
April pp 33-48, 110

ELECTION DAY ACTIVITIES
November pp 83-92

ESKIMOS
January pp 83-94

F
FAMILY AND FRIENDS
June pp 47-60

FATHER'S DAY
June pp 39-46

FEATHERED FRIENDS
May pp 63-82

FIRE SAFETY
October pp 75-82

FLAG DAY
June pp 33-38

FLOWERS
May pp 26-28, 32-34

FOURTH OF JULY
July & Aug. pp 46-54

G
GROUNDHOG DAY
February pp 29-36

GROWING THINGS
April pp 75-88

H
HALLOWEEN
October pp 83-100, 106-109

HANUKKAH
December pp 93-100

HARVEST ACTIVITIES
October pp 20-23
November pp 19-32

HEART ACTIVITIES (HEALTH)
February pp 83-93

I
INTERNATIONAL CHILDREN
CHINA - January pp 66-67
ESKIMOS - January pp 92-93
GREECE - April pp 94-95
HOLLAND - December pp 82-83
INDIANS - November pp 41-42
IRELAND - March pp 48-49
ISRAEL - December pp 96-97
ITALY - December pp 76-77
JAPAN - March pp 92-93
MEXICO - December pp 70-71
PAC. ISLANDS - June pp 92-93
PILGRIMS - November pp 39-40
RUSSIA - May pp 30-31
SWEDEN - December pp 90-91
U.S.A. - July & Aug. pp 42-43

J
JAPAN ACTIVITIES
March pp 85-96

K
KING, DR. MARTIN LUTHER
January pp 71-81

L
LIBRARY ACTIVITIES
November pp 61-72, 107-108

LINCOLN, ABRAHAM
February pp 37-46, 99

M
MASKS
October pp 45-56

MAY DAY
May pp 29

MEXICAN INDEPENDENCE DAY
September pp 81-88

MOTHER'S DAY
  May pp 37-51

N
NEW YEAR'S DAY
  January pp 49-56

NUTRITION
  July & Aug. pp 71-84

O
OCEANOGRAPHY
  June pp 83-100

OLYMPIC ACTIVITIES
  April pp 89-104

P
PILGRIMS
  November pp 33-50

PIRATES
  June pp 95-100

PLEDGE OF ALLEGIANCE
  November pp 90

PRESIDENT CARDS
  November pp 92-100

R
REPTILES
  June pp 63-82

S
SCHOOL BUS
  July & Aug. pp 93-94
  September pp 34

SEASONS
  January pp 33-48

SKELETON
  October pp 57-66

SNAKES (REPTILES)
  June pp 80-82

SOLAR SYSTEM
  July & Aug. pp 55-70

SPRINGTIME ACTIVITIES
  March pp 21-34

STATES AND CAPITALS
  November pp 73-82

ST. PATRICK'S DAY
  March pp 35-52

SUMMER ACTIVITIES
  June pp 21-32
  July & Aug. pp 28-33

T
TEETH (DENTAL HEALTH)
  February pp 73-82

TESTING
  May pp 104-110

THANKSGIVING
  November pp 28-32, 33-60

TRAVEL AND TRANSPORTATION
  July & Aug. pp 85-96

TURKEY ACTIVITIES
  November pp 51-60

TURTLES (REPTILES)
  June pp 63-82

V
VALENTINE'S DAY
  February pp 47-62

W
WASHINGTON, GEORGE
  February pp 63-72

WEATHER ACTIVITIES
  March pp 53-72
  April pp 30, 31, 108, 109

WINTER ACTIVITIES
  December pp 27-30
  January pp 19-32, 100-103

WOMEN IN HISTORY
  March pp 73-84